HOG RANCH
BY MATHENGE
MAY 1995

H. Mathenge
May 1970

Dik-Dik / Hog Ranch front lawn

ZARA'S TALES

ZARA'S TALES

from Hog Ranch

Perilous Escapades in
Equatorial Africa

PETER BEARD

ALFRED A. KNOPF
NEW YORK
2004

THIS IS A BORZOI BOOK
PUBLISHED BY ALFRED A. KNOPF

Copyright © 2004 by Peter Beard
All rights reserved under International and Pan-American Copyright Conventions. Published in
the United States by Alfred A. Knopf, a division of Random House, Inc., New York, and
simultaneously in Canada by Random House of Canada, Limited, Toronto. Distributed by
Random House, Inc., New York.

www.aaknopf.com

Knopf, Borzoi Books, and the colophon are registered trademarks of Random House, Inc.

Grateful acknowledgment is made to Paul Simon Music for permission to reprint an excerpt
from "Kodachrome" by Paul Simon. Copyright © 1973 Paul Simon. Reprinted by permission of
Paul Simon Music.

Library of Congress Cataloguing-in-Publication Data
Beard, Peter H. (Peter Hill), [date]
Zara's tales: perilous escapades in equatorial Africa / Peter Beard.
p.   cm.
Contents: The darkness that may be felt—*Funga safari*—Big pig at Hog Ranch—Roping
rhinos—The man-eaters of "Starvo"—Lake Rudolf—This is reptile country—The fate of the
pebbleworm—The truth comes through the strangest door—Under the mists of the Kenya
snow—On the run.
ISBN 0-679-42659-0 (alk. paper)
1. Africa, east—Description and travel—Anecdotes. 2. Africa, East—Social life and customs—
Anecdotes. 3. Natural history—Africa, East—Anecdotes. 4. Animals—Africa, East—
Anecdotes. 5. Beard, Peter H. (Peter Hill), [date]—Travel—Africa, East—Anecdotes. 6.
Beard, Peter H. (Peter Hill), [date]—Homes and haunts—Africa, East—Anecdotes. 7.
Photographers—Africa, East—Biography—Anecdotes. I. Title
DT426.B43 2004
967.604'092—dc22   2003066118

Manufactured in Singapore
FIRST EDITION

The naked mole RAT

For Zara

Tsavo Man-eaters 1984 on the Galana

CONTENTS

THE DARKNESS
THAT MAY BE FELT

"Why did you first go to Africa?" people always ask.

And I never know what to answer. Was it the hand-painted screen in my nursery, zigzagging around the cagelike crib with its towering giraffes, in the heart of New York? Palm trees and scatterbrained monkeys that separated my two brothers and myself from spitball fights and roughhousing? Or was it the Walt Disney drawings on the wall of Bambi, Pluto, or Dumbo flapping his big ears, getting ready for takeoff?

I had a hand-painted plaster-cast rattlesnake, menacingly curled up in some leaves in a wastepaper basket, that held endless fascination; and a mossy aquarium where salamanders and newts lived in damp contentment—and every spring, in the country, there would be garter snakes, turtles, tortoises, snails, squirrels, chipmunks, and sometimes raccoons and possums who trapped themselves in the garbage. I craved it all.

"Keep your animals out of the house!" my mother would bark at me four or five hundred times a week. But the animals were all that interested me, and they always ended up indoors.

I remember watching a small box turtle, captured on Ocean Avenue, Bayberry Point, Long Island, eating a bit of raw hamburger in the garage. This held my attention for hours. What was going on in that very old-looking head? *Chomp, chomp*, with its steady round red eyeballs that blinked periodically with camera-like precision, a tiny red lens seeing, focusing and blinking, staring out from its shell, with its armorplated legs, tiny toes, and a minuscule tail. Here was a living machine, chomping food right beside our lawn mower, leaving lumpy puddles. The slow mechanical leg movements, the hissing retreat into its garage-like shell—the whole magic package unchanged for hundreds of millions of years—intimations of vast tracts of time and the miracle journey of evolution: the survival of the fittest, the infinite variety of species, the ingeniousness of the natural world.

It never occurred to me that these natural day-to-day wonders weren't the most meaningful, mysterious, magic reminders of all Natural History and of whatever it is that's lurking behind all living things: plankton, plants, palm trees, pythons, peacocks, parrots, pigeons, Pygmies, pigs, possums, pandas, pumas, panthers, plovers, platypuses, puff

adders, prairie dogs, prickly pears, pumpkins, parsnips, parsley, pimentos, pack rats, porcupines, peccaries, puffins, pelicans, penguins, pintails, porpoises and polar bears, everything—a dark universe waiting for someone brilliant to explain it all. Where did all this stuff come from and where did *that* place come from?

When I was six, I saw Gargantua, the famous gorilla in the Ringling Brothers and Barnum & Bailey Circus, under the Big Top in Montgomery, Alabama, in tornado weather. A year later we moved north to New York for school, and there was the gigantic Grand Central Station, Atlas holding the world on his shoulders at Rockefeller Center, and there, too, on a rainy day, was the great Natural History Museum on Central Park West with the huge wet Indian standing out front next to President Teddy Roosevelt, the father of Conservation, sitting tall on his giant horse, muscles bulging and gleaming. All enormousness.

Inside was the great African Hall, with a darkness you could feel. A gorilla family in the lush forest, the big silverback standing up beating his Congo-drum chest, jungle vines, hidden snakes, dried bones, twigs, tick birds, African driftwood, all inside. I stood there in the dark, by the railing, gazing through windows into that other world. Over my left shoulder, in majestic silence, was a herd of elephants, ears straining forward, trunks outstretched, sensing danger.

Maybe that's why I first went to Africa? Perhaps my African journey began in that dark hall.

New York City in the mid-1940s still had trolley cars, open double-decker buses, organ grinders' monkeys running around with tin cups asking for coins. One single Indian Head nickel paid the bus driver then.

Morning after morning, year after year, I saw my face reflected darkly in the ninth-floor mail chute outside apartment 9A at 133 East 80th Street after a breakfast of runny eggs, soon to be dumped out the back window when no one was looking. On my way to school, waiting for the elevator, my dim reflection in the mail chute looked like someone else staring back from another time, a darker continent, looking through the black chute—a stranger wondering why it was so dark, so quiet, so hard to see. Such grimness, seeing someone seeing someone seeing someone in the cold light of dawn. Then a mad rush of mail would shudder by, an in-house waterfall causing the chute to vibrate, and the elevator cables to groan. This was my every-morning school-day routine day after day for seven years.

To focus in on brighter things—brighter than homework—photography became a way of life, a way to preserve and to remember the passing, changing, fast-fading favorite things: bullfrogs, woodcocks, ruffed grouse, ducks and deer, weekends and summer vacations with my dog Charcoal. Snakes from the woods, moist neon orange salamanders with chartreuse spots revealed like tiny jewels under moss-covered

rocks, freshly laid frogs' eggs from the murky swamp, tadpoles, polliwogs—jars full-to-go, with ice-picked lids for breathing holes. All were mystic reminders of what people called Natural History. For me it was paradise with campfires, axes, knives, traps, traplines. I wrote to the Northwestern School of Taxi-dermy, for a first lesson in preservation. Saving the game! Wildlife! Pho-tographs! Honest-to-God subject matter! I wasn't old enough to draw, so what could be easier? *Click . . . click!* I lived for the glossy results, for that moment of tearing open the yel-low Kodak envelopes and submerging myself in the frozen frames, the new realities, life-thickening windows on-to a captured world that beat the rush of time. Even the accidents were fresh, new and welcome: bad expo-sures, double exposures, wild move-ments, high-speed flukes, light leaks, lost focusing—learning to appreciate these exciting mistakes was part of the magic. And, into the bargain, it was a rather tricky way of getting ani-mals into the house.

So, finally, maybe I went to Africa to photograph the errant wildlife, *the wild-deer-ness,* the wild unspoiled Stone Age connectedness of the place. Primitava! Exotica! Authentica! Crawling creatures, creativ-ity, biology, ecology, anthropology—it was all there: "a continent of wis-dom, dignity, and deep poetry, equally expressed in nature, beast, and man."

I had to find out what it was like to *escape* the drudgery of Mondays-back-to-school, delinquency, demerits, detention, dehumanization; to step into another time, to experience the open spaces, the "endangered species," the Big FIVE: lion, leopard, buffalo, rhino, and elephant. The enormous isolation, the impersonal solitude, the joy of escape, the need to set sail . . . RELIEF in a world without socks or underwear!

It was amazing to discover this otherworldly world where the laws were very old and common sense was still a strong ingredient. Suddenly

I could plunge into a way of life where survival wasn't just an expression. It all happened so naturally, accompanied by the music of mourning doves, the cries of the crimson-winged turacos, tree frogs and cicadas singing to me. The Dawn of Man was all around me. And the feeling that I'd been there once before would come to me.

Crocodylus niloticus, a particularly scaly Nile 'dile, low in the water . . . *click* . . . *click* . . . caught as he slithers by as he has for the last 170,000,000 years.

On another level I probably went to Africa for fun, to get away, to grow up, to graduate from graduating, to fulfill my dreams, to learn something new from something old. I came face to face with the truth that we too are animals, rather dangerous, territorial, and greedy, but animals all the same. And if I just stayed out there in Kenya for a while, I could do books about all this. So when I was still a student, I went to Kenya, to the vast continent of Africa, bought forty acres of Mbagathi Forest on the edge of Karen Blixen's coffee plantation, and promptly lost myself in a child's paradise. I put up a tented base camp there and called it Hog Ranch, after the clans of bristled warthogs that lived all around, and still do. This has been my base camp for over thirty fast-moving, explosive, dramatic, surprising, shocking, frustrating, exhilarating, primitive, satisfying, down-to-earth, animal-ridden years.

Eventually I got married and had a daughter named Zara, which means "yellow desert flower" in Arabic—a little dark-haired evolutionary beauty, an old soul, with an age-old brilliance shining through, a brand-new surprise, a born storyteller herself. The tales recorded here

are for her and for her friends (and for you too, dear reader), to thumb through one day. Tales to induce dreams about the Big Game *NYAMA* (in Swahili—the word also means "meat").

Yes, the time has come now to slow down and dream dreams about the old world, the wild life, the wild animals, and the wonderful things we may or may not have left behind.

And as this world shrinks and turns and changes in front of your eyes, try and remember that what I've put down here is true and that Nature's truth is always greater, stranger, more complex, and more incredible than mankind's make-believe.

Lala salaama	Sleep well
Watoto yetu	Children
Kesho jua tashona	Tomorrow the sun will shine
Kwa heri ya kuonana	Good-bye and see you soon.

Your first lesson in Swahili has begun.

. . . Nature I loved; and next to Nature, Art.

I warm'd both hands before the fire of life;

It sinks, and I am ready to depart.

—WALTER SAVAGE LANDOR

THE PARAMOUNT CHIEF KINYANJUI

FUNGA SAFARI

*F*unga safari! is the cry you hear when it comes to packing up and leaving for an African trip or, as it so happens in this case, leaving Africa itself—now that humans outnumber wildlife by thousands to one, and the last refuge has been invaded. *Funga safari!*

In the old days it was off to Athi River, Darajani, Kitani ya Ndundu, Galana, Dakadima, Ndiandaza, Kathamula, Garbatula, Rumuruti, Ruhuti, Muringata, Mweiga, Magadi, Moite, Loingalani, Alia Bay, Koobi Fora, Uaso Nyiro, Tana, Masongaleni, Simba Station, Kikumbuliu, Loliondo, Loita—magical singing names that flood the mind with associations, of adventure, of nostalgia for a long-gone past, a raw, beautiful nature. So *funga safari*, pack up your things, pack up your kit and leave . . . *the thrill to be on the move is as fresh as ever.*

Then, of course, at some regrettable point, the expedition loses momentum and inevitably the need arises to turn around and head back to town to deal with those repulsive realities—like looming lists of things-to-do, licenses, permits, dentists, lawyers, immigration, insurance, supplies, repairs, and corn for the hogs at Hog Ranch.

"There is no world without Nairobi's streets."
—KAREN BLIXEN,
Out of Africa, 1931

Nairobi, the old railhead, the place of cold water, in Masai, was always a chilly comedown at time of re-entry. Years ago it used to be a quaint, eccentric pioneer place, full of characters of all stripes and tribes, individuals, hunters and travelers, and those taking the cold water.

Wildlife was in the streets. Lions walked down Government Road in 1953. A rhino rubbed itself on the District Commissioner's office, scattering its dung all over the front stoop, like a black rhino should. Local residents went to the movies in their pajamas. It was fun. Thirty years down the road, romantic Nairobi evolved into Nairobbery. Grew big and busy and touristy and started becoming just like everywhere else. It was full of geeks and gorms in bullet belts and leopard-skin hatbands, police and army personnel, UN types, do-gooders, and insipid immigrants like me. *Escape* ran like an invisible banner across the narrow smelly streets.

Tab. XLVII

Verres   Eber

Aper   Wild Schwein

Scrofa   Mock

Escape was everyone's number one business and more currently is everyone's frantic need.

So, "what-to-do?"—the famous Indian railway workers' lament when the Tsavo man-eaters were snatching them night after night from their tents. *What-to-do!* Exactly what I used to mutter and agonize about when it came time to *funga safari kwa rudi tena* (to pack up the safari and return to town—Nairobi).

To solve this problem pickle, to fix it so that I was never *off* safari, never indoors or far from a glowing campfire, I put up some tents in a patch of bush twelve miles outside of Nairobi. The place was suitably populated with warthogs, waterbuck, bushbuck, suni, dik-diks, leopards, giraffes, and occasionally buffalo or lion, along with my best friends, nomads and bundu bashers (*fundis* of the *porini*), all feeling at home.

Mbuno and Galo-Galo, two veteran trackers from my safari days, came from Machakos and Voi. Mwangi and Kamau were Safariland skinners with Mau-Mau backgrounds from up-country. Mwéma and Kivoi Mathenge were both artists and cooks, *mpishis* trained by Kamante Gatura, who had prepared Karen Blixen's meals from 1921 to 1931. Kamante and his wife Wambui lived with me at Hog Ranch from the very beginning and brought to it a real feeling of the Old Africa, the *earlies*, the early days, when things were simple. Not easy, but simple.

And this is all I ever longed for: the atmosphere and natural pace of the old days, which show up so clearly in those scratched and faded early films; haunting exposures of savage enormity, Stone Age space, sepia-colored "authentica"—worked on by specks of dust and the scratches of time. The feeling still shows up sometimes, in the darkness of dawn, in the great quietness and loneliness of the tropical nights when hyenas come and the wild dogs howl.

The feeling of standing out there, alone under the nocturnal enormity—the shooting stars, like tears on cheeks, run down the sky and disappear. This endless sky, where the Southern Cross hangs above the iron gray wasteland of the plains, the plains of midday mirages at Ongata Rongai. *Darkest Africa*, which means only that its timeworn roots were

Loibon Taiyana son/of *Ol Lenana* ... *with his father's rhino-horn rungu*

not exposed to glaring, blazing, blinding lights, *pitiless as the sun*, aimed at darker, calmer eyes. Such thoughts come to you in the deep, intoxicating, isolating nights of equatorial East Africa.

At home at Hoggers, around the open fire before the sun disappears behind the Ngong Hills, I sit with Zara and watch all the warthogs finish their day of rooting around and gobbling up corn and bran in front of our tents. Then, in single file, they waddle off to the deep holes they have dug for themselves, very carefully hidden away in the forest floor on a steep slope leading down to the Mbagathi River.

The Mbagathi is merely a small stream that dries up between rainy seasons. It separates Ongata Rongai, the open plains of the Masai, from the densely wooded Mbagathi Forest, Kikuyu country, where, in a clearing on the upper ridge, the Hog Ranch tents are pitched.

As if to a silent signal, we gather by the fireside in deep violet-blue twilight just before dark, the best time of day, when everything magically settles down into silence. Kivoi and I are drawing in books and pasting photos into diaries, filling in the gaps, now and again looking toward the shadowed hills, the birthplace of the Masai, sharing stories of the earlies and failing to get squirming Zara in the mood for bed. A tiny bird, the robin-chat, is bravely claiming his tree, calling out the last chirpy notes of a long, hot equatorial day. Zara's hedgehog Tiggy squiggles past along the red-earth floor, nosing here and there for scraps. Deeply resonating roaring and rasping grunts come up from the forest valley like a giant saw going back and forth on a dry log. It's a leopard, signaling the night.

For many years, long ago, *zamaani sana*, as they say, this very place was a famous battleground in the struggle between Masai warriors (the famous blood-drinking spear-throwing tribe of fearless lion hunters) and their age-old enemy, the shadowy Wa-Kikuyu, who lived in the shaded shelter of the woods.

Many fiery hot-blooded warriors were killed in these borderline battles, and one enormous grave of piled-up rocks marks the final resting place of an old Masai loibon, chief or medicine man, who must have been speared or clubbed to death right here where we now sit so cozily.

African travelers, passing by, throw stones onto the hero's grave out of respect. Zara has frowningly accepted my explanation that the stone throwers do this to gain from the bravery of the fallen leader (much as the Irish kiss the Blarney Stone).

Not to do it would be to risk *bahati mbaya* (bad luck). So she gets her stones and pebbles ready in advance.

On moonlit nights we often walk to see this grave, squarely positioned on an ancient, rock-hard, worn-down cattle track from which we have an inspiring view of God's Knuckles, the four small summits of the Ngong Hills, overlooking Hog Ranch and the vast stretches of Masailand, and the Great Rift Valley floor, far below.

Just before everyone's bedtime, out of the forest and up the hill a family of giraffes float past our open tents like shimmering ghosts in the moonlight. Every year, there are more houses and less forest, so the giraffes are always hungry for an extra evening meal of the special bran on which our hogs have been pigging out all day.

Graceful and fluid, like slow-moving large creatures underwater, they stoop to empty the bird feeder. Up in the treetops, the small furry tree hyraxes scream at each other—*Aghhhhhhhhh . . . Aghhhhhh.*

I amble slowly by with Zara fast asleep in my arms, her head heavy against my shoulder, her mind now occupied in other worlds of dreams, possibly of Thaka, the warthog, *giri yake;* or the hyrax, *litole;* the squirrels, *msongereri;* the flocks of tiny finches, *ndege nyingi;* and now, just beyond her exhausted reach, the towering giraffes, *twigas, mrefu sana,* with their long dark purplish tongues licking up the last of the birdseed, making a silvery dream of themselves, heads bowed against the outline of the Ngongs.

An olive tree reaching twenty feet overhead is delicately nibbled as an owl swoops past. Miragelike, the giraffes melt away in the nighttime, a downhill parade, through thorn trees to the water holes of lower Hog Ranch.

The campfire flickers, sparks fly up as Mbuno turns a log. The hills stretch and spread. You can sometimes feel another dimension hovering here, just within your reach . . . in this great, bottomless, bottle green, underwater world. Time slowed to infinity before the white people came. We float along in helpless motion, in an ageless, endless, dreamland aquarium of all nature. It's as if I went from a time of keeping those animals out of the house, to a time when the house opened up to encompass the African plains, and all the animals in it.

Mbuno and Thaka

BIG PIG
AT HOG RANCH

The biggest warthog that was ever seen at Hog Ranch was named Thaka by admiring friends. He weighed over three hundred pounds, had stubby legs, and his hair stuck out in all directions like a worn-out brush. He was first befriended and slowly encouraged to visit us by Mbuno and Kamante, who for years had lived at Hog Ranch and knew exactly what to do. They patiently lured Thaka (Kikuyu for "Handsome Fellow") nearer and nearer with special corn and leftover bits of barbecued chicken.

With food in hand, they would make little grunting pig noises in the back of their throats and sit down quietly whenever Thaka emerged from the bush at the edge of the forest.

His upper tusks were long and polished from daily foraging. Hidden underneath were shorter, thinner tusks, razor-sharp ivories for fighting rival pigs, African dogs, or the Mbagathi Forest leopards, who seemed to prefer pigs and piglets to any other meal.

Thaka soon became Top Hog. Everyone else would get out of his way. He was the leader and protector and the main show-off, the wise one, the number one heavy at Hoggers. Others would have to stop and tremble when Thaka sauntered in. Only humans could frighten him. He seemed to own all the territory around us.

In the early mornings, when he first emerged from the cold, dewy, low-lying bush, he loved a really vigorous tummy rub, especially in those tender spots under each leg where little ticks might be hiding, out of reach. We came to learn about this weakness from a one-eyed vervet monkey that lived in a tree next to the main tent. Kamante named this little monkey Northi-chongo, the One-Eyed, after old Governor Edward Northey of Kenya Colony, who had lost an eye playing polo when Kamante was a boy.

Early one morning, right there on the front lawn, all alone, Northi-chongo was grunting and grooming and looking for friends to de-louse. When he discovered that the smallest piglets quite liked his company, he started grooming them, emitting his rhythmic monkey-mouth clucking noises. That's when thuggish Thaka entered the picture and took over, claiming all the attention for himself. When Northi-chongo commenced picking the bugs off him, he kneeled down and rolled over, groaning in ecstasy, eyes closed, pleasing his newfound monkey friend as well as getting pleasure himself.

From that time on we always knew more or less who liked what and from whom—how, when, and why. Whenever Thaka saw us emerging from our sleeping tents, he would dramatically roll over, keeping a squinting eye on us, waiting and hoping for his really ridiculous tummy tickle. This is where Zara comes in, because she always needed someone to play with—and who else had all the time in the world? Zara eventually persuaded Thaka to plunk down, in a sideways falling-over collapse, at the first sight of a potential tickler—such as herself!

It was hard to resist such a grand gesture from so cunning a swine. Thaka was clean and warm to the touch. After a good rubdown and scratching, Zara's fingertips would smell like hickory-smoked bacon.

Never to be forgotten was the evening when, just before curfew (near 7 p.m.) when all the hogs disappear like clockwork downhill into their holes for night, without warning of any kind, a very bristly-haired wild-looking boar hog sauntered onto the front lawn, attracting the attention of Thaka. Our personal pig was lying down in his favorite position: munch, munch, *munching* from a very big pile of the finest cereal bran nicely organized by Zara for this late-evening meal. Then, like a shot from a cannon, Thaka exploded forward from munch level, straight at the hairy intruder, hair up everywhere . . . and right in front of the guest tent, their two brutish bristling heads crashed together.

For the first time in my life, I saw the unleashed power of the wild pigs, the amazing bullish strength, tension, and strain, head to head, pushing, shoving, squealing, jostling for the better position, tusks locked together; then abruptly coming unlocked, slashing each other viciously with deadly moves faster than the eye could follow; then *WHAMMING* their heads back together, crashing and spinning, not to mention ripping apart the garden area between the tents, and snapping the tent ropes and the whole gamut from *BASH* to *CRASH* to *SMASH*.

I yelled "Thaka!" at the top of my lungs, again and again, hoping to interrupt the deadly fight. But it was like whispering at an avalanche.

Message from Northi-Chongo

The intense concentration and determination and sheer power of the combatants was scary. Zara raced forward to be near her closest companion. She cried out in shock and terror and had to be yanked back into safety. By now, great bushes had been knocked down and trampled. Half the guest tent was down. Skid marks from desperate hooves scarred the whole of the front lawn.

Kivoi and Mbuno, who were watching from the kitchen porch, rushed out with buckets of cold water and we threw them on this fight-to-the-finish. The hogs took no notice. Ten minutes became twenty. We poured more and more cold water, now from only a few feet away—three or four buckets at a time. But it had absolutely no effect on this grisly territorial combat. Everyone feared for Thaka. Both pigs had hurt each other. Death for one or the other seemed inevitable.

After endless time the battling boars bulldozed into a patch of thick bush downhill between small trees. I jumped onto some lower branches, swinging down and kicking into the fight, pulling up at the

early Hog Ranch

very last second to avoid the slashing heads. After about five attempts, this weird scheme suddenly worked. The bloodied heads unlocked and parted. There was a split-second pause, and then the stranger bolted off, never to be seen again.

Thaka stood there, gasping, hurting, brutally shaken, dazed, head sunk low. He was oozing blood. It was dark all around him. He was standing in another world, a world of animal pain. He did not move. I didn't dare go near him and had no choice but to leave him alone in the failing light.

For the first and, we suspected, the last time, he would be late for bed.

Zara's face was wet with tears. We cleaned up the battlefield and tied up the tent as best it could be. After a comforting fireside meal of soup and toast, Zara was put to bed. She fell into a restless sleep, not knowing if she would ever see her favorite pig again.

That night lions roared and grunted till dawn and the ever-hysterical hyena contributed his chilling whoops.

But to bring in the sunrise there were cinnamon-breasted doves, cooing their song. And cawing combative turacos swooped through the fever tree vines, making flashy landings and scuttling off through the criss-crossed branches. Yesterday's scattered birdseed attracted nervous crowds of tiny finches, firebirds, indigos, and cordon bleus. Mbuno arrived at our tent flap: "*Jambo! Hodi. Habari? Chai. Thaka bado kuja.*" (Good morning. Greetings. How are you? Here's your tea. Thaka has not come back yet.)

We sat up in bed, watching some helmeted guinea fowl chase each other around the tents. Nervous tree squirrels jumped from place to place, scampering out of the way. A mongoose darted across the lawn, tail arched high over his back—hiding against hawks, rushing to a secret egg supply buried under the kitchen. Kivoi was outside, drawing pictures for this very book. Mwangi was sewing up pig-inflicted damage to the guest tent. Several small oinkers trotted out for breakfast. Zara couldn't stop herself from asking questions about Thaka.

"Where's my Thaka? Will he come now?"

None of us dared answer.

Clutching a cup of tea and an orange, I carried her to the acacia tree house built by Mwangi. It helped cheer her up to be sitting up there so high above the forest. We looked out over the hills, the four Knuckles of God, the birthplace of the Masai, the blood-drinking tribe of lion hunters.

The sun was hot overhead now. A crested eagle circled in the valley below. Several giraffes could be seen down in the forest, just their heads nibbling in the thorn trees. A lazy tree hyrax hopped across a clearing and came to rest under the Land Rover.

It was one of those hot quiet mornings, nothing moving, nothing changing. And there, right in the middle of it all, down on his knees in his favorite feeding position, was Thaka, Mr. Casual himself, grazing in the center of *his* Hog Ranch.

Everyone had been watching for him. No one saw him arrive. With Zara on my shoulders, calling his name, we rushed to greet him. As if on

cue, he plunked himself down and rolled over with a sigh of expectation. His wounds were so beautifully covered over with mud, they couldn't even be seen, and they didn't seem to bother him at all. Zara stared wide-eyed, amazed in gratitude.

As far as Thaka was concerned, nothing out of the ordinary had happened.

It was just Africa, after all.

ROPING RHINOS

Darwin's great-grandson + White Rhino

There is always something
new and strange, out of Africa.
—PLINY THE ELDER

Farther down south in Zululand, Umfolozi's park warden was constantly talking about having far too many of an animal that was far too rare—too much of a good thing. On one moonlit night on an open plain, he saw sixty-four white rhinos standing together in the silvery glow—a horny mob scene under the full moon. He was observing a slight indication of an oncoming population explosion. These nearly extinct relics of the early world were so protected and were multiplying so fast it was getting scary. They were overgrazing the limited land, overeating it, slowly but surely exceeding the carrying capacity of their shrinking territory. If something wasn't done soon, there wouldn't be enough for any of them, and that is the sad dilemma that this part of Zara's book addresses.

S. Serengeti: last two rhinos

In Africa, there are two kinds of rhino: black and white. The black one is smaller, about five feet at the shoulder, very short-tempered, unpredictable, and sometimes dangerous. When in doubt, it blunders forward, huffing and puffing in the direction of the enemy—like a hyperactive tank. Otherwise it browses off bushes, chewing leaves and branches, scattering its dung to mark off territorial boundaries.

The white rhino is calmer and grazes on grass with its square-looking lawn mower lips.

The Dutch settlers called it *wijd* (which means "wide" but sounds like "white")—wide-lipped for pulling out the grass. The largest bulls are six to seven feet high at the shoulder. They graze like cattle, behave like gentlemen giants, and never scatter their dung. Just as I say never, I realize that once, quite by surprise, we did film one huge *wijd* rhino standing on his territorial dung heap back-kicking his droppings furiously with both hind feet. But then animals love to break the rules laid down by foolish man.

The world's last stronghold of wild *wijd* rhinos is way down in the southern part of Africa, in Umfolozi and Hluhluwe ("Shish-loo-wee," when you read aloud), Zululand. On my way to Kenya in 1955 I visited these two sanctuaries with a fellow filming fanatic from school. He also happened to be the great-grandson of Charles Darwin. So it wasn't that long ago that Darwin gave us his theory about monkeys and men.

By 1961 I was out of school and up north in Kenya, East Africa, for good. The white rhino dilemma down south had become *six years more serious*. Finding new homes for these crowded creatures who had once roamed the whole continent suddenly became a panic program and a full-time job for the warden. There were many offers from zoos, but for him confining animals unnaturally was not the answer. Kenya was the answer: open, spacious, and perfectly suited to his overpopulated pachyderms. Politics and transportation from south to north were the only obstacles. Lots of black-and-white red tape everywhere.

After years of wrangling and bickering, it was almost decided that Kenya would cooperate by trapping and trading some of its black rhinos

galo-galo + ele-eaten tree

for white rhinos from Umfolozi. Years and years went by. Finally, it was confirmed that Kenya would trap some of its black rhinos and exchange them for the ones with lawn mower lips from Shish-loo-wee. With all the official paperwork and international eco-mania, it took eight more years for the first white rhino to arrive in his crate at Aberdare National Park headquarters in Mweiga, near Nyeri, in the famous White Highlands of Kenya.

So truth comes through the strangest door. Because of that summer safari with the white rhino warden long ago (1955), I now had my first and favorite job in Kenya—roping rhinos.

While the paper pushers were wrangling numbers in Nairobi, we were playing real live high-speed animal games in Ukambani, wildest Wa-Kamba country, Darajani-Kikumbuliu, near Mtito Andei, bouncing around on the running board of a Ford Bedford catching truck, tearing through the baobab and commiphera forests of hunting blocks 28, 29, and 33, large protective buffer zones around Tsavo National Park. This was the big game indeed. "*Engawaaa . . .*"

By pure luck, the Kenya Game Department had hired the most eccentric local animal trapper in the history of this eccentric calling—my next-door neighbor, Ken Randall, a gnarled and weather-beaten veteran of Old Kenya. It wasn't long before his junkyard generators, dead Jeeps, spare trucks, rusty engines, torn-up tires, animal crates, catching pens, and shagbag sheds full of who-knows-what spilled over onto Hog

Ranch. Untold acres of overflowing paraphernalia, along with gas tanks, jerry cans, spare tents, and tools: I found my place invaded by a collection of former Game Department workers, or *watu*, shagbags in tattered rags of bush-ripped clothing.

Ready or not, on the morning of our eventual departure for the rhino-infested Tsavo lowlands, we got up while it was still dark, clambered into the most dilapidated vehicles ever wired together, and headed south on the Mombasa road, 150 miles into hot and humid baobab country.

We camped on the Darajani River near a place called Kikumbuliu on an old hunting track, seventeen miles in from Mtito Andei—"the place of vultures"—where so many dead bodies rotted away when the Great War came to Kenya and the German general Paul von Lettow-Vorbeck's Ruga Ruga troops outfoxed the British, 1914–1918. Kikumbuliu was a Wa-Kamba name on the old nineteenth-century maps in the middle of the densest bush imaginable. This was the "interminable jungle" described by railroad engineer J. H. Patterson. Here I pull out an old signed copy of Colonel Patterson's turn-of-the-century account about the man-eaters of Tsavo. Patterson spent ten months tracking down two maneless man-eating lions whose appetites had brought the building of the Mombasa railroad, the "lunatic line," to a grinding halt in 1898. The map in the diary-book shows Patterson's Tsavo Bridge camp just a short distance from Kikumbuliu.

Now nothing was there but us and the ancient ghostlike baobab trees that shaded our tents and Randall's ramshackled rhino pens. In a few years all this would be gone, but for the moment it was pachyderm paradise.

We were working for Conservation! catching rhinos in the hunting blocks, releasing adults in the National Park, and saving small ones for Southern Africa. We were the gardeners of Eden!

Kamante Gatura, companion and cook from Karen Blixen's *Out of Africa* days, and Galo-Galo Guyu, the once-great Waliangulu poacher and Mau-Mau tracker, were with us. Our sleeping cots were set up near the rhino pens. When rhinos were brought in and had recovered from the roping ordeal, they began hammering at the commiphera-log walls. All night long the noise would grow louder and more violent, until it became very frightening. No one but lunatic Randall, who thrived on dangerous chaos, got any sleep. Although the logs were dug deep into the ground and were wired together with enormous crossbeams, the strength of an adult rhino could never be guessed. At night we left Petrolax lamps burning to keep the rhinos company, but they slammed into the commiphera logs like crazed behemoths. *Hell-bent for horror.* Another and another resounding *CRUNCHHH* . . . desperate to find a loose log, a loose anything, any way out, any escape from the man-made nightmare.

Ken Randall had a very ornery sense of humor and he liked things that really bent other people's minds out of shape. Once we caught a beautiful little rhino for Tsavo Tsafaris, a national park campsite twenty miles away on the Athi River. It was a favor to Glen Cottar, the third-generation professional hunter who built the camp that year. His grandfather, who was killed by a rhino on the Tanganyika border, had come to Kenya at the turn of the century from Cottar's Creek, Texas.

The baby rhino we caught for Glen had already been fed a week or two of rhino vitamins; antibiotics; vigorous de-ticking and de-worming, complete with coconut oil rubdowns; milk bottles; and delicious yum-yums like sugarcane and candies; and at last the spoiled brat was ready for Glen's area, tame as could be. A great ceremony was at hand. Tsavo's proud warden was in attendance with his impeccable rangers in their Mowgli-green national park jungle suits, shiny boots, and berets. So there was quite a little crowd when the bouncing baby, christened Rudi, was finally about to be released into his brand-new playpen at Kitani ya Ndundu, "the hiding place of both poacher and owl."

But Rudi was reluctant to leave his cozy, crated quarters; lots of candy had to be held out to coax him our way. A great number of tooth-some sweets were slipped into the front gap of his prehensile mouth to get him interested in moving. The warden's rangers had never seen anything like this. They gaped and giggled with every bonbon handout. One smiling neophyte ranger gripped some candy himself, peered at it, and

sidled over to Rudi's outstretched lips. Like a nervous schoolboy called up in front of assembly hall with the entire student body watching, he held out the offering.

The trick is to put it right in the center of the mouth—there's a gap there—*quickly.*

His timing must have been a little off, because before you could say Jack Robinson, his hand was yanked from Rudi's jaws with one finger missing—gone, neatly chewed off at the base. Blood spouted all over a puzzled Rudi, who was still chomping away happily on the ranger's lost bit of anatomy. More blood also flowed down the man's freshly pressed, Mowgli-green khaki uniform. He just stood there, with a puzzled look. Dead silence. Fellow rangers rushed in to help him. There was a little huddle of help. And then, possibly half a minute after bite-down, a sort of tumbling thud was heard from the driver's side of the release truck. And there—rolling on the ground, shaking and gasping, tears of laughter streaming down his face—was Ken Randall, our leader, the crazy Kiburu (South African for "Hairy Back").

It was this laughing-in-the-dirt lunatic who was to plan the day that forever remains Zara's favorite story.

During many long months we were limited by Game Department decree to catching only very young rhinos. The difficulty of spotting such a minority group from the ground, endlessly trucking through thick bush, meant running into the quarry by sheer blind luck—and it took forever. Ropers and spotters were on the lead truck. Following behind was ambush vehicle No. 2, with a gang of diggers, pullers, spare ropers, and general helpers. It was a large group slogging hundreds of miles through dense scrubland. All hands (Africans) were extra sharp in eyesight and local knowledge. But the resident black rhinos in a wild hunting block are perpetually scared and always on the run at the slightest sound of mankind closing in.

Day after day we bumped along from dawn to dusk. No matter how hard we tried, we could never convince Randall to use light aircraft to spot the hidden rhinos—or to take a bath! "No, it just won't work," he would mutter, wiping even more grime across his weathered forehead.

First priority was avoiding burnt-out baobab stumps. These were charred open holes—vast black pits left over from local bushfires, sometimes twenty feet across—into which an entire catching truck could fall with a backbreaking crunch. On the chase at 40 mph, special spotters were appointed to watch out for these killer caverns while crazed and nutty Randall floored it through all the other nice little surprises like blind gullies, termite hills, boulders, rocks, acacia stumps burnt black and hard as steel, plus miles and miles of suicidal madness—like extra-thick walls of concentrated woodland into which Ken loved to hurl his truck at whacko speeds. Absolutely flat-out in a tight pinch, he would choose to run over not-so-small smaller trees, aiming, with a kamikaze grin, his reinforced steel bumper and nailing the whole thirty-foot-high grove square into the ground in a split-second rush of wildest exhilaration.

Of course, he had no side windows left, and the windscreen had completely shattered years before—so the driver's compartment filled up with the leftovers of everything he ever hit. That left very little room for Randall. The filth in there with him was fearsome.

About a month before roping finger-eating Rudi, Ken had promised us that he would take a bath, a really big thorough wash, when he brought home his *next* young rhino. He looked and smelled as if it was a year too late. Then, on the actual morning of Rudi's unforgettable capture, in the 110°F Ukambani midday heat, caked with dust and engine oil and gundge from untold weeks of grimy truck-repair-filled rhino-roping days, exhausted from the race against the heat for home, Ken plunked himself down in the shade of his chaotic mess tent with a chipped and cracked cup of orange squash, squinting dusty eyes, staring into space, puffing on some locally made Rooster tobacco, thinking out loud with satisfaction.

"Yup," he sighed. "I think I *will* take a bath . . . when we catch the *next* rhino."

Loud groans of despair came from all around the mess.

When official word got to us that we could now go for rhinos of all sizes, Ken decided on the biggest one possible. He had glimpsed it from time to time over the years. It was an enormous silver-backed bull that lived along the Athi River near Masongaleni. Its silver color simply came from chalky dust baths, but this Moby Dick of rhinos would truly challenge Ken's mania for darkest peril.

I am always careful to explain to Zara that these adult rhinos got disinfected and de-wormed plus receiving all kinds of good treatment and special favors before they were turned loose again, sometimes eighty miles away, deep inside Tsavo National Park. The bad news was that the National Park sanctuary, over eight thousand square miles of wild woodland, was being eaten to the ground by a ravenous horde of about forty thousand overpopulated elephants, themselves victims of our own human overpopulation, pressing in on them *from all sides*. So we were actually "rescuing" rhinos from a lush, green hunting area and releasing them into an overeaten, windswept wasteland, a man-made Elephants' Graveyard. This is the logic of bureaucracies and politicians heroically engaged in "saving the game," from their fund-raising offices. The good news was that this righteous release into Armageddon in no way stopped the beasts from walking right back, *mara moja* (first thing), to their old home grounds, lush with browse, and very green, near us in Darajani. So all's well that ends well. This was Conservation at its loony best.

The waste of time was immense, but the way of life was rich. To make matters totally ridiculous, depending on one's point of view, the Game Department's scouts who camped with us as official "spies" studied the folly of the mysteriously returning rhinos. They wrote copious notes and *never said a word*.

Ken Randall was the man for the job. Wildlife translocations without any harmful tranquilizing drugs—new homes for all. Extra-smelly or not, he knew rhinos better than anyone and he had an uncanny animal instinct for understanding the fast-evolving world around him. He worked with a vengeance, fully committed, lost in speed and thunder, mad-crazed on the trail of his four-legged, armor-plated, tanklike friends.

> "Without passion there is no truth."
> —KEN RANDALL

And so the wildest day ever spent with Ken was basically a madman's gift to my camera and to Zara's Hog Ranch storybook: chasing the big one, the silver-backed bull that he had secretly always wanted to capture. Just for the hell of it, "to test the rigging," so to speak. There was, of course, no sane reason for the hunt—a petty credit for a South Africa exchange, perhaps; a release-credit on paper in some office—and surely

Ken Randall in his prime

the guaranteed return journey for a fully educated rhino who knew perfectly well on which side of the park border his bread was buttered.

Like many things in life, it made no sense; it just happened—from one committee meeting to the next.

One morning, in the darkness of dawn, we all set off for the big one. It was near Christmas. Everyone was in high spirits. Kamante Gatura had outdone himself: pan-fried *posho* (hominy grits) and fringe-eared oryx liver, swimming in gravy, with freshly baked safari bread, damp in the middle. For once both trucks were working well. In the darkness and warmth of the Tsavo lowlands we motored happily along a seldom-used track toward Masongaleni.

The sky went blazing red from purple. Miniature dik-diks, all delicate fragility, rushed around in pairs. Some lesser kudu saw us coming and vanished in a flash of twisted horn and flippant white tails. Hornbills called out to each other, nagging and gossiping. Helmeted guinea fowl were flushed into flight. Great elephant herds were moving away from the Athi River as the sun came up over the Yatta Plateau. No flat tires yet.

As we motored along the open track, our festive mood was shaken by an interruption from the roper's side of the truck. Eighty yards away

Rarely seen Lesser Kudu (Tsavo)

the bushes parted and without warning, in broad daylight, a furiously fuming, snorting steam engine at full speed came bearing down on us. So far, no problem, as this is standard rhino behavior. A big bluff right to the very end of the charge and then the brakes will suddenly be jammed on and the front section goes up high, head and horn knifing the air with snorting explosions in mid-arrest. *But not this time.* This one was really steaming—full locomotion, full motivation, full tilt! Total hate at the sight, sound, and awful smell of us. A rhino express train that never slowed down at all. Even Randall agreed he had never seen anything like it. It took less than ten seconds for the brute to reach us. An immense crunch. The catching truck shook like Jell-O in a thunderstorm, a tiny tin toy torpedoed. Minds were racing. What charging beast could survive such an impact? We braced ourselves for the blood-torn horn, brain damage, a skull cracked wide open. But no, to everyone's adrenalinized amazement, this thick-head just turned around and trotted off with a casual shake of its monumental dome.

Everyone piled out to check the steel siding. A dent the size of a tree trunk had been gouged into reinforced steel. By now the rhino was too far away to consider a chase, so we drove off on full alert for anything else that rustled.

Within minutes there was an urgent knock on Randall's roof. Galo-Galo had spotted a speed-runner, a rhino huge and "silvery," in the distance. Switching gears, we roared into full throttle, hearts thundering: you wait months for this. Quickly goggles go down and the holding bar behind Randall's head is gripped securely by one and all—for dear life, believe me. You could hear trumpets and bagpipes. Without conscious thought or pause to think, *the race was on.*

Our truck flew through the bush unlimited. On its own, truck No. 2 swung left and right, roaring, everything suddenly happening at lightning speed. The engines racing, gears grinding, branches flying. Standing just behind the driver's cab, the roper aimed his lasso tied onto a bamboo pole. With every turning, skidding, crashing through trees he re-aimed the bamboo—otherwise it would have snapped in pieces or been torn away. The ropes were ready. Branches streaked by, ripping. Spare tires flew. Trees snapped down. Overlapping sounds in colliding collage, *ahhhgrhhaaahh* and beyond.

Randall threw his truck through two-wheel turns and cut the distance, thinking far ahead. The rhino ran, head held high, at full speed, knowing every hole and gully. He disappeared on turns and went up and down in full control. The huge bull was, undeniably, way ahead.

Truck No. 2 was out of sight. No ambush plan can be thought of in this madness of sound and speed, of grinding gears, backbreaking bumps, bodies flung up and down. More speed from the Captain's cab, more jarring bumps, the groaning of steel, our gripping knuckles shaken white. Waves of branches and rubbish filled the cab. A punctured tire meant nothing now. Randall is way out there—into do-or-die. A true maniac unleashed at speeds impossible to slow down—loving it. Out on a limb of chance, the bullfighter's dream, the impossible odds. The die is cast. One last wrong turn, a hairsbreadth away from the burnt-out baobab. Skid right, race ahead, shift gears, gun the engine, jump it, turn it, tear away, crash through: now or never.

Truck No. 2 was doing miracles. Suddenly the rhino was in between the trucks. Now the roper's noose was down. He was leaning forward outside the racing truck, way beyond good luck. More tension builds. Closer and closer . . . for a mile or more. A mad dash left, the rope rips off the pole—*Fix the pole!*—a final open stretch ahead. The trucks on either side, the noose dropping down again, the rhino staying ahead, the loop dangling along its silver back. Branches whipping at man and beast. Too fast, too rough, too much, only inches away . . . try for the neck or even the legs. Lose balance. Noose down, ready, head or foot—bump, crash—*Kamata! Kamata!* (Catch it!) Rope it, try it, lose it, wave it over, under now, the rope tantalizingly near, nearer, down too far, both trucks together, off the pole! *No! No! Fix it! Go! Go!*

A miracle. The rope falls perfectly—

Head, horn, ears, neck, the rope rips off the pole. The men take turns and loop the post.

Rope! Rope! A host of hands grab it. It whips out at ripping force and smoking speed. The wood post screams with rope burn. There is a shout for *Water!* Water is poured, steam and smoke. The rhino bull is spinning,

spearing, kicking. There is a shout for *Leg ropes!* Screaming, frantic, chaotic moves. Two men are out with ropes—*Funga! Funga!* (Tighten the ropes!)—*Get that leg!* Dust clouds, the rhino spins on a dime, everyone jumps away—Bellow, snort, crash the bush, slam the truck, a close call for Linga-Linga the roper, the runner, the giant Turkana. Randall is on the running board, yelling like a banshee, two ropes on and tied, now a third, two or three around the neck. *Angle the ropes! Pull the legs—Up! Up! Up!* At last three legs are looped. Randall jumps behind the truck.

I'm under the truck out of reach, camera clicking. The rhino horns a tire (*click*), all ropes tighten, opposite legs are pulled up. *Sukuma!* (Push!) Three miles, three ropes, three legs, take a turn—*again and again. Sukuma! Frūta!* (Push! Pull!) Frenzied *furūta*.

Down he goes, his head still crashing up and down, six feet high and then smashing down, snorting dust. Explosions. *The bag! Get the bag!* A burlap pillow goes under the crashing head, a bag of sawdust crunched a hundred times cushioning the unbelievable impact. Shovels and picks are out.

It was a race against time to dig a five-foot hole through roots and rocks . . . *Deeper! Deeper!* It had to be deep enough to back the truck down in to let the beast be pulled on board. Sometimes it took twenty minutes, sometimes more. *Pull together now* . . . Roll rhino onto wooden sled. *All hands together—Ahh-bé, ahh-bé frūta sasa!* (Pull now!) The animal was on its side, straining, heaving, throwing its head over and over again . . . until the ropes snapped and flew away. The animal was almost on its feet again, incredible—*Run away / Run back / More ropes*—heavy snorting, breathing, gasping, thumping, choking, and groaning in the equatorial midday heat. Shovels and picks broke more rock-hard ground. Randall brought jerry cans of water for his fallen charge. A precious pause to load more film. The truck backed down and filled the hole. *Ahh-bé, ahh-bé, frūta kabisa sasa!* Pull it all the way—all the way up!

All aboard! All tied down. Ready for home. A symphony orchestra was needed now, or maybe a soaring chorus from Handel with the Vienna Boys Choir, to underscore our mad race home. We were speeding up to catch the passing air, as in a speed breeze. "They can't stay on their side

Linga-Linga, digging the truck in

for long," Randall kept yelling, revving the engine and shouting Swahili curses. The truck hit 50 mph on the straightaway. Under low trees, the babbling congregation in the back bowed down in unison, zooming home, a thundering crescendo of organ music. Ken Randall has lost only one rhino in his life. The Kenya Capture Committee lost ninety-nine from overdosing and mishandling. *All this was Kenya Conservation.* Save the rhinos! Save the Game! S.O.S. Save our sorry souls.

Racing along the last stretch, down the steep hill, sharp left to the Darajani River crossing. Our camp in sight. *Open the doors . . . logs aside . . . clear the hole!* The truck backs down the hole. The rhino sled pulls off. *Ahh-bé, frūta kamba!* (Pull the rope!) Watu heaving on the ropes. Into the pen. The sled is in. *Get the door! More wire! Funga kabisa baba! Funga! Funga!* Fasten completely. More logs are brought and wired into place.

Injections . . . ointments . . . antibiotics—*dawa* (medicine). Everyone is working quickly. Ear tag. *Toa kamba!* (Release the ropes!) *Toa sasa!* (Untie the leg ropes—now!) The heaving rhino lies there, stunned, a burlap blindfold on his face. *Clear out! Pull the blindfold!* All hands and feet race for the wall. *Water!* A bucket of water splashed over the dazed beast. The ground quakes. *My God, he's up again!* Wobbly, staggering, snorting, heaving, rushing the wall. *Crash, bash,* spin and turn. Searching for the enemy. *Kwenda wéwé?* (Get out!) *Look out! Go away!* Again the horn slashes. "Clear out," Ken mumbled. Leave him alone. We have him. *Wacha wéwé! Kwenda! Kwenda kabisa.* Let's leave him alone.

This is Zara's favorite tale. She likes it when the big one is breaking the ropes and the tires are horned! I hid under the sinking truck and then, at long last, Ken Randall actually took his idea of a bath—a quick dip in the Darajani River, which Zara knows to be full of nibbling shrimps, squiggling, creepy little bugs, and amoebas.

THE MAN–EATERS
OF "STARVO"

It is hard not to become addicted to the warm, intoxicating rhythms of the Tsavo lowlands. Tsavo North has been a closed area since the park was opened in 1948. It has a dangerous reputation. No outsiders went there. It was rugged beauty and isolation unequaled. Dawn-of-man doum palm sunsets, dramatic colors that you might see only once in a lifetime. Dusk and dawn. This was Wa-Kamba country, Ukambani, the ultimate in atmosphere, complete with darkest Africa's nighttime noises, tree frog symphonies along the riverbanks and up the luggers: twenty- to thirty-mile-long dried-up riverbeds like Pleistocene sandboxes. When Zara was three I took her there just to have her experience the greatest playground in history and to dig deep water holes in the dry sand.

Elui ℀ nzenge

By day it reaches 110°F, too hot for more than a *kikoi*, a cloth wraparound, and Pitamber Khoda slip-on sandals. This was the home of Waliangulu and Giriama hunters: beekeepers, trappers, and trainers of the batteleur and the Gilles crested hawk eagle, the dark chanting goshawk, Augur and honey buzzards, Verreaux's eagles, and Lanier falcons. Waliangulus were daring bowmen, fearless hunters of rhinos, and the biggest tuskers in Africa.

Long ago, this was the home of the notorious man-eaters of Tsavo. Now, with its overpopulation we call it "Starvo." Maneless lions feasted off railroad workers and were known to snatch sleeping passengers from their costly Pullman berths in the dead of night and make a disgusting meal of them. Tsavo had the wildest of wild dogs, giant elands, the tallest giraffes, jeweled chameleons, scorpions as big as lobsters, the world's longest spitting cobra, the one-ton

the crested hawk eagle

elephant-skull fungus (a great vegetable from the elephants' graveyard), delicate long-necked deerlike gerenuks that never drink water, Peters gazelles, the bat-eared fox, and the naked mole rat, a squinting sausage with teeth, that never emerges from its underground tunnel systems. This revolting rat toils furiously underground in massive antlike colonies hundreds of yards long. It lives an insectlike existence, complete with pregnant queens: yet another haunting message from Charles Darwin and the origin of our species—all the strange connections between different kinds of animals and insects through the untold centuries.

But now we were living in the 1960s. Kenya was about to achieve independence. In twenty-five years Zara would be born. Out of untold millions of years, it would be the last twenty-five years of wild and free rhinos at home in the East African bush. Whenever Ken Randall shut down his rhino rescue operation and traveled up-country for supplies, rest, and recuperation, Galo-Galo and I journeyed downstream to Kitani

Kathamula on the Tiva sand river: female gerenuk dazed at midday —

ya Ndundu to visit Rudi the rhino and help Glen Cottar with his Tsavo North foot safari area—*for the more adventuresome visitors,* as his brochures would say. Galo-Galo and I were building natural-looking rock blinds at water holes to serve as overnight fly camps, places safe from lions and elephants. In our spare time we were also gathering elephant photographs for a special double issue of *Life* magazine, December 1967 (and Glen's Nairobi posters). It was to be a last look at unspoiled Africa—"The Wild World," as *Life* called it. The text was by Romain Gary, his famous letter of apology to the elephant: "In my eyes, dear Elephant, sir, you represent to perfection everything that is threatened today with extinction in the name of progress, efficiency, materialism, or even reason. . . ."

We followed the elephants with cameras, even at night, all through Tsavo North, from Dakadima to Ndiandaza, and along the Athi-Tiva to Ithumba and the hunting block beyond. We had a permanent campsite on the regular Tiva, a sand river, a dry lugger, at a sort of elephant-highway crossing known as Kathamula: a primordial place where Africa was still breathing in its ancient natural rhythms. Very few people had ever been there before. Decades later, when Zara finally visited this paradise, it was still untouched. She lost no time digging herself a number of sandbox-sized swimming pools from which her friends the great elephants could drink later on that night.

That's the way it was for her and me, night and day, a child's dream, a distant archetypal memory that can only be conjured up on old forgotten films. I can still see and feel my broken-down 1960 Land Rover on early morning river runs, driving down the prehistoric riverbed through assemblies of quietly rumbling elephants going about their eternal business, unaware of their imminent appointment with destiny. I watched them feeding and watering, framed in my viewfinder between doum palms, digging deep water holes for us and for the lesser game in the scorching months before the long rains, before the cattle and the locusts.

I can always re-feel my months there, so alone except for Galo-Galo Guyu, the best silent guide in the world. It was an idle time of full-moon

blind construction, night stalks through buffalo herds, past solitary bull elephants with a hundred pounds or more of ivory on each side, and many, many rhinos (always scary escapes in the dead of the night), of basically never getting out of a *kikoi*, of learning where to find the last bit of usable water, trap birds, start fires, call out to owls and eagles and others. All of which marks me as one of the lucky few who "have lived in the best of times and seen the wonders of wildlife and belong to a brotherhood which has memories that cannot be matched . . . we have lived on into a new world which I do not pretend to understand" (from a letter to Teddy Roosevelt by Alfred Pease, an ostrich farmer outside Nairobi, 1908–1909).

Galo-Galo was born near Voi, a hundred miles away in the small community of Waliangulus. *Waliangulu* is the Giriama word for "Meat-Eaters." They were traditional hunters, renamed "poachers" by us. They were first discovered and employed as elephant trackers by such

George Eastman and Philip Percival on safari in Nyeri, 1920s

Denys Finch-Hatton

great white hunters as Bror Blixen, Denys Finch-Hatton, and Philip Percival, who was Teddy Roosevelt's personal hunter in 1909. For centuries these bow hunters lived, and lived well, among the elephants and rhinos. A natural order was established—coexistence—symbiosis! They were all surviving nicely, in balance until the white man came along *to save them*. The whites staked out protective boundaries, arrested the hunter-gatherers and upset the balance. Concentrated populations of reproducing pachyderms overpopulated and overate their food supply. Disaster was then at hand.

Like other Waliangulu hunters, Galo-Galo was a master bushman. During the dry season, when water was out of easy reach, he would fash-

Bror Blixen, 1927

Photographs by Thomas Dinesen

ion a six-foot drinking straw from reeds to sip up the subterranean treasure. Games and puzzles, traps, snares, bows, beds, bags, ropes, fires in the rain—he knew and could make them all, anywhere in Ukambani. Watching him was an education which I needed for survival in the Tsavo bush, the *makori;* the lowlands, the *mustoni,* the *nyika.* Whatever hardship, Galo-Galo adapted quickly.

~ Sisal leaf

Once, when he and I made a citizen's arrest of a wire-noose-snare setter who had trapped a small suni, a local judge convicted *us both* and handed down two one-and-a-half-year sentences plus twelve strokes with a cane. The case was retried and eventually the decision was reversed. During our gloomy incarceration in Kamiti Prison I had missed a sleeping mattress and edible food; Galo-Galo never complained.

On safari, there was no better companion than this quiet hunter, trapper, humorist, and humble friend, always in tune, in touch, in harmony with his surroundings. He lived with the game, kept the balance, did his honorable best. His was an authentic life of risks gladly taken with few wants or needs, intellectual in ways both practical and artistic. And most important of all, he led a life in which man does not become a plague on his environment.

One day, after a spell of following up elephant bulls in the Athi-Tiva area, where the biggest tuskers seem to gather together in what are called *bull areas,* Galo-Galo and I were getting "sand happy" from prolonged isolation and pure independence from the rest of the world when a visitor who had lost his way motored down the track. He was a genial Kenyan-born bone-digger named Robert Soper, whom I never

galo-galo guyu

the drawing); another spot is in front at the foramen of the
trunk, and lies somewhat above the line forming the two orbital
cavities. A third, but seldom accessible, is above on the roof of
the skull, whilst a fourth lies on either side, behind the aural
foramina at the back of the skull. These spots being thus
defined, a great deal depends on the direction in which the
bullet strikes, and an exact knowledge of the formation of
the skull as well as a sure eye and a steady hand are essential
to ensure success in hunting these animals.

88   THE DISCOVERY OF LAKE RUDOLF

SKULLS OF AFRICAN ELEPHANTS.

But we must get back to camp now. The valley in which
we had halted ran on for some distance further, but was much
encumbered in certain portions; we therefore crossed the
base of Mount Nyiro at the beginning of the next march. The
volcanic plateau facing Mount Nyiro on the west gradually
increases in height further on, and becomes merged in
lofty highlands, also of volcanic formation, which present a
perfect chaos of wild ravines and perpendicular precipices.
After a march of many hours we reached the somewhat less
rugged northern end of Mount Nyiro, finding it to form a ridge

saw again but who does live on as the only
other eyewitness to a midnight fright-night
incident so dark and sudden I can only tell it
to Zara in the daytime.

This nightmarish jungle tale happened
after a long day spent digging up an elephant
skull out of the Tiva sand and leaving the great
divot as a gift waterhole. We had also, very
miraculously, found some ancient ochre-clay cave drawings on the eastern face of the Yatta Plateau on a rocky slope under a cliff face, before the
track goes up and over to Cottar's Camp, thirty miles away.

Toward evening, exhausted, worn down from the heat, we were
back at fireside under the whispering doum palms that line the Tiva in
great clusters at Kathamula. From the supply chest, Galo-Galo magically
produced a great, green bottle of Japanese rice wine that we had forgotten to celebrate the New Year with, time and timelessness ticking by.

There were Ritz crackers, bread-and-butter pickles, Hellmann's mayonnaise, and some sort of yellow packaged soup to feast on. With all the sake, we celebrated an equatorial feast that night.

Robert Soper was quite relieved to have stumbled on our camp. His food reserves were low and to make matters worse he'd just been researching Colonel Patterson's early accounts of the marauding man-eaters of Tsavo, the beasts who actually stopped the making of the Mombasa railroad by hunting down Patterson's labor force—not that far from where we were camped.

Soper told us that the lions were said to be the ghosts of nature, immune to bullets and able to rise up against modern man's intrusion, and that they had grown fond of human flesh—of that there was no doubt. He had heard it was the lack of salt down in these lowlands that caused them to develop their taste for smelly, sweaty railway workers. Or maybe it was just the shallow graves of the casually buried victims of blackwater fever and malaria. A full twenty-eight of Patterson's men had been taken by these "Devil Lions," ambushed and brazenly dragged away, often devoured within earshot of their friends.

The three of us were drinking the warm sake at fireside. The night wind was up and blowing through the palms. Several hours of typical Tiva pleasantness and prehistoric sounds and hot tropical darkness slipped smoothly by. In the Tsavo heat that had turned our crate load of

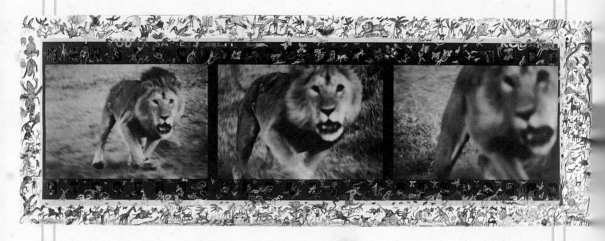

I could plainly hear them crunching the bones, and the sound of their dreadful purring filled the air. They had doubtless indulged in the man-eater's habit of licking the skin off so as to get the fresh blood. On two half-eaten bodies the skin was gone and the flesh looked dry as if it had been sucked.

—J. H. PATTERSON, *The Man-Eaters of Tsavo*

Fanta orange drink into the color of gray dishwater, the after-dinner conversation switched to guessing games about the centuries-old ochre art from the Yatta Plateau—slightly drunken wild ideas of what it may have been like to actually be there then, alone and lost in time with cavemen and nighttime beasts and superstitions of every kind.

As the mostly liquid meal stretched sociably into a moonless, windy night, I received a call from Nature and just had to go, walking forty feet from the bright fireside into total blackness to settle my business. Without a thought in my mind, as carefree and ultimately brainless as I will ever be, I stood there staring blankly into space, performing my natural duty.

It came in slow motion, like a bullet train erupting out of a tunnel, soundless, without any sense of reality at all. The fireball express at midnight. Like an ancient force, a primitive power, bigger and more powerful than you or I can ever imagine—an unnameable and unbelievable flow of silent *SPEED*—a mental nightmare before I knew about it, like

when you get burned and snap back before the pain registers—and so much more. I stood paralyzed and overwhelmed. And then I let out one humongous yell, from the depths of my sun-stroked soul, a scream as primal as his charge, so loud that I believe Robert Soper may have wet himself at fireside. My friend Galo-Galo sprang from nowhere and kept up the yell . . . and in a slow-motion predator-cat weirdness, as silent as the whole episode, this monster lion became a man-eater with brakes. Dust was everywhere. And Galo-Galo was beyond me with daring motions, while I began to realize what was happening and in the next second . . . as quickly as it came, the glorious gray devil was gone.

The only thing that remains in my memory, like a red-hot rivet driven home, at the exact instant my stomach went up through the back of my neck and into my brain, I know it and will never forget it—that we are all carcasses in the deepest sense. In essence, *flesh is grass.*

Thankfully, this was the last man-eater we ever had for dinner.

the End

We traversed again the dreadful jungle (of Tsavo) where we frequently could scarcely see the sky. After we crossed the River Tsavo we entered a still larger wood where my people would have lost their way completely had they not climbed tall trees from which they could discern the snow-capped summits of the Kilima-Kibo and Ndara.

—J. L. KRAPF, December 1849

The Ukambani woodland paradise came *pole pole* (slowly slowly) to a point of no return late in the 1960s. There were very few trees left in Tsavo National Park. The ancient baobab forest and the seemingly limitless commiphera woodland that stretched forever were being pushed over and gobbled up by too many elephants. Too many of the Wakamba and Waliangulu traditional hunters were imprisoned, shot, or banished for sticking to their old ways in their own homelands: *hunting with bow and arrow*. That's how they had kept the balance for centuries. Now the park, once thick and green, looked like a battlefield of driftwood, twisted and dusty. Enormous pressure had been brought to bear. No longer was the problem of conservation saving one or two thirsty orphans. The urgency now was saving the environment.

> In my eyes, dear Elephant, sir, you represent to perfection everything that is threatened today with extinction in the name of progress, efficiency, materialism, or even reason . . . It seems clear . . . we have been merely doing to other species, and to yours in the first place, what we are on the verge of doing to ourselves . . . my longing for your company is actually a nostalgia for my long gone innocence and childhood. And, indeed, you are precisely that in my eyes: a symbol of purity, a dream of paradise lost, a yearning for the impossible, of man and beast living peacefully together.
>
> —ROMAIN GARY

Tsavo—you should rename it Starvo—was a clear warning of an overcrowded, denatured Africa. Overpopulation and mismanagement became key issues worldwide. Density and stress-related phenomena

Nguya & his 201 lbs Nile Perch
speared at high noon / Alia Bay
Lake Rudolf · September 1968
(for Eyelids of Morning
the mingled destinies of crocodiles & men)
1964–1968 population dynamics
study of the last undisturbed
population of the Nile crocodiles
in existence (now no more) –

caused major die-offs—not to mention wars—around the shrinking world.

So, with the last of my *Life* magazine elephants safe in their slide boxes, I said farewell to Galo-Galo, Kamante, Mbuno, and everyone at Hog Ranch and set out on another journey, five hundred miles north to a lake full of crocodiles in the middle of a *real* desert.

Arriving at Ferguson's Gulf in the sizzling mirage of midday heat waves, I joined biologist Alistair Graham at his base camp, on a mission for the Kenya Game Department. He was working on a population study concerning the last undisturbed population of Nile crocodiles, detailing the facts of their lives, hoping to demonstrate some useful purpose to their existence before expanding numbers of humans exterminated them with spears and fishing nets. They had lived undisturbed for aeons in this Pleistocene lake, itself almost as old as time and once part of the Nile.

This gigantic glistening "Jade Sea," lying on the floor of the Great Rift Valley at the end of the Omo River, is a watery jewel, set in over 530 miles of desolate, windswept shoreline in northernmost Kenya, smack up against Ethiopia and the Omo River delta. It's a fearsome place of volcanic rock, smoking craters, and dark, windblown sand, home only to wild and wooly nomads. *This* is the Northern Frontier. Hundreds of thousands of years ago Lake Rudolf was connected to the River Nile. Now it is cut off, with a dropping water level, at what seems to be the end of the world. It seldom rains. Hot dry winds blow day and night, first from one direction and then, after lunch, from the other. Temperatures reach 120°F.

Ahead of us were years of hard work—hunting, stalking, collecting, and carving up crocodiles; checking their insides; charting the complex facts of their lives. We lived and traveled with the nomads that passed through this forlorn paradise. Our chores were arduous. The site was brutally harsh and haunting. Still, as paradox would have it, the dry and dusty desert days turned out to be healthy, humorous, and totally splendid.

It was a round-the-clock adventure. We never knew what to expect next. One night our boat, *The Curse*, named for a never-ending run of bad

The ancient Greeks called them Kroko-drilos, "pebbleworms"—
scaly things that slither and lurk in low places. But man gets on
with crocodiles about as well as he did with dragons, and just as he
did with dragons, he will banish them from all but the remotest
parts of the earth.

—*Eyelids of Morning: The Mingled Destinies of Crocodiles and Men*
New York Graphic Society, 1973

— specifically told not to go swimming —

luck, broke her moorings and drifted for miles away across the lake. On four other occasions she sank in heavy storms with us on board, and on the fourth she sank for keeps, sucked into the immense waves of Alia Bay. But that's another whole horrible tale.

Later, our friend and research partner Mulji Modha, on Central Island, right in the middle of the lake, would be grabbed from behind by a ten-footer that brought two thousand pounds of jaw power to bear on his bum. After a grisly tug of war, helped by an assistant who was literally *pulling for him*, he managed to crawl away. "Flying Doctors" took him home. He was eventually admitted to the Ahhhgah Khan Hospital, Nairobi, with massive bite wounds.

One moonless night in a 40 mph gale on North Island, cut off from the rest of the known world, Alistair Graham was bitten by a spitting cobra. He jumped aside at the last fraction of a second so that the fangs only lightly grazed him. You could see the two tooth marks a few centimeters apart, and from each minuscule wound came the tiniest trickle of blood. Over the ages this cobra's long-gone relatives must have floated down on bits of driftwood, all the way to North Island from the Omo River delta in Ethiopia forty miles away—a chance of one in a million of getting marooned on this totally remote island. Alistair's twenty-minute walk back to camp was full of chilly uncertainty. We all waited for the fatal agony that would signal his end. But it never came.

Murille, Rendille, and Boran night raiders, independent and menacing nomads, would pass our campsites in the dead of night, stop to peer at us for a few moments through the dark and howling wind . . . and then go away.

Sometimes our tents flew away—blankets, beds, anything, everything, got caught by the infernal howling wind. We had to have specially designed blow-through canvas shade-makers rigged up on steel frames. Everything had to be anchored down with iron pipes, sledge-hammered in. Finding firewood was a major chore as there were almost no trees. Rudolf was getting hotter as well as windier.

Over the many months our teeth turned brown from drinking the alkaline lake water that tasted like melted jellyfish, until we imported special acids and dropped them into water-storage jars. This helped sink the gundgy goo, leaving bland, slightly awful, but drinkable water.

We ate gale-blown black volcanic sand in every mouthful of food: catfish, perch, turtle, zebra, whatever. Hyenas and lions stole and ate quite a few of our fresh croc carcasses even though we anchored them off-shore, tied underwater with rope. Scorpions crawled into our Pitamber Khoda sandals. Damp-skinned toads crawled under every jar and metal box. Poisonous nighttime carpet vipers hung around camp, waiting, and made wandering barefoot a kind of guessing game.

Here we were, all busy scratching around in the burning volcanic sand on a successful Easter egg hunt, Turkana-style, tracking down chirrupps, finding the eggs, and then witnessing some spectacular baby croc births. Alistair was wrestling with dozens of these babies, filling charts with lengths and weights and drawings of the tail-scale clippings—marks made for future identification of each growing individual—all entered meticulously into my diary.

Ebei catfishing off croc carcasses

The embryonic crocs had tiny, temporary, pointed horn-growths on the top of their noses for breaking through their leathery eggshells. This little tool-gift from Nature gave them a shortcut out. To help them further during their first difficult days of croc life, a yolk sack of food was sticking out of their scaly bellies. Few animals start life so small (eight to nine inches) and then grow in just fifty years to be *fifteen, sixteen, seventeen, or eighteen feet long*—in the end, a real dragon of a reptile, weighing several thousand pounds. About 170,000,000 years back, evolution had designed a fearsome little survivor. For an animal to have lasted on Earth for this long makes us think twice about our own brief history of two or three million years and our uncertain chances for the stressful future.

We found that the average number of eggs laid per nest was just over thirty. The bigger and older the females, the more eggs they could lay. The world-record clutch, sat on and hatched by one big mother, in Uganda, was *ninety-five eggs*. How the babies actually manage to produce such loud noises, CHIRRUP, CHIRRUP, from inside their shells, sealed off from the air, is a continuing mystery. But the protective mother, swimming around nearby, hears these cries and helps by digging up her young ones at just the right time. A twelve-foot mother will dig up her chirrupping eggs and, with greatest delicacy, crack open each shell with her massive teeth. Out pops a diminutive baby—her spitting image, fangs and all.

She proceeds to carry a mouthful of babies down to the water to save them their first risk-filled journey across a hostile beach. Hyenas, iguanas, gulls, and other crocs present a full range of enemies.

Nguya, a most cheerful El Molo *moran*, warrior, from Loingalani, had joined our party for the sheer adventure of it. He had narrowly survived a gruesome raid when Somali bandits with automatic rifles shot up the local fishing lodge where he worked; they killed a visiting Catholic priest and shot Guy Poole, the manager, in the back of the head in Banda 6 and, finally, speared and skinned an unknown Italian driver. Rumor has it that several of the *shifta*, bandits, were later seen wearing bits of the Italian's skin as decorative trophies.

We were having a glorious day digging away. Eggs that weren't quite ready had to be kept at the same angle at which the mother buried them, and then they would hatch for us later. If they were turned around in any other way they would die. We were very careful. Each was marked.

Looking around, I noticed Nguya had moved off into the reeds a few hundred feet away. He was standing there stone still, peering into the soupy warm water. Was he bored with the egg hunt and the peculiar palefaces who were digging it—with pencils and pads, clippers and scales?

He was used to us by now, adjusted to our weird ways, so what *was* he doing out there? Gusts of wind were flattening the reeds around him. Alia Bay is one of the windiest places on the lake, but Nguya was somehow immobile, motionless—absolutely rigid, frozen in his place against the inestimable elements. Waves lapped against his dark legs as if against dock posts driven into the ooze of the grimy bottom.

I became more and more curious at this statuelike display. But Nguya wasn't bored; in his own way he was intensely busy. I could just detect his hands moving, *pole pole*, an eighth of an inch at a time. He was locating the end of his doum palm root rope and slowly snaking it around his body. Then, with only the fingers of one hand, he tied a knot, securing the rope around his chest. Suddenly he stood there like an Olympic javelin thrower, spear raised, rope carefully organized, poised for combat.

The wind was coming from behind him. His leg moved. He was leaning way back now in intense frozen concentration.

Then . . . everything went into the throw. No more than fifteen feet in front of him the shaft of his flimsy wooden spear drove down into the murky, wind-whipped waters of the lake.

An explosive geyser of spray erupted with such amazing force it looked like someone's airplane had nosedived into the drink. It was unbelievable. What monstrousness could that be in the shallows?

We were stunned, for as quick as the throw was unleashed, Nguya vanished in a tidal-wave burst of water that seemed to swallow him up. Was he crazy enough to try a full-size croc with his single baby-toy spear? It seemed so.

Dropping baby dragons like hot potatoes, we ran down the lava beach, already mourning a drowned friend—diary abandoned, pages madly flipping, machine-gunning in the Lake Rudolf desert wind.

Back then I had never seen the power of a nuclear sub under way, making a huge bow wave out in front, big enough for Hawaiian surfers. But on the lake we were still living in the Stone Age and Nguya's wave had a whole new frightening energy.

The mind-bender was plowing along in deep water now. It was far ahead of us and we were running like demons, an emergency rescue team, out of breath . . . gasping . . . adrenaline pumping. My friend, the spearman, is drowning! His corpse would be dragged down, dead weight, lungs full of water. No more lectures on cozy living around the lake of plenty. No more loony squeals of laughter as he teased a baby scorpion into someone's itchy burlap shirt.

The great driving wave was slicing through the choppy water and then it turned into a new cove of rougher seas. We ran. Needle-sharp spiny spike grass with piercing blades stung our bare feet. We were fly-ing along, as fast as possible, puffing and panting in the highest heat of the day.

I don't know how long it took—just an eternity. We slogged around another bend, all black rocks now, and *there he was*, sitting in the water, ALIVE, Nguya our pal, laughing, giggling, talking to himself . . . no

croc . . . no legs missing . . . no problem! "*Naona hapa*," he cried. "*Naka-mata samaki*." It was just a fish . . .

Nguya was "saved" by anchoring his feet in hippo-hoof-holes at the bottom of the water (which at that point, he says, was only waist high).

Like a kid with an outsized pet, Nguya pulled his braided leash while the enormous prey wallowed against the power of his thin El Molo frame, both arms and chest heaving, legs jammed into the gooey lake floor. He had speared a bloody great Nile perch! He had been aiming for the gills but the iron end of his spear was a bit off target—high and back—and so he got a high-speed ride out of this slight error.

We had to stay away while he patiently eased the monster bit by struggling bit into a dead-end cove of jagged lava rocks. It was at least 200 lbs of edible *samaki*. Nguya weighed 140 lbs at most.

Another twenty feet in toward the rocky shore and the fish looked gigantic in the shallows. The dorsal fin on top fanned out in deadly warning. Its mouth was like Jonah's whale: you could crawl in there and get lost. Its eyes were golden neon beams of cool cold light, perfectly round and glowing up from under the brackish brown slimy sulphur-smelling water as if from the bottom of the world. Here was evolution itself, ashore—like the distant cousin of some prehistoric fish pulled up through an ocean hole, a traveler through the tunnel of light and time, with all the age-old energies, flopping at our feet.

We dragged the monster out, its scaly giant rear end still protesting, its yellow eyes glaring, and its gargantuan mouth gulping ancient despair.

That afternoon, we weighed the pieces bit by bit. It was definitely over 200 lbs. A new record for us, and tasty too. It lasted for many Hellmann's-enriched meals by the lakeside.

Some small time later, the Nairobi *Nation* ran a snapshot of another Nile perch. It had come from Lake Victoria, from the very bottom, dragged up in a commercial fishing net, winch straining, Africans amazed. Its weight: 700 lbs. Our friend Nguya was not impressed—*his* had been caught in single combat. Then he added with toothy grin: "How could one eat so large a fish?"

THIS IS REPTILE
COUNTRY

So the warm and windy months of croc research went by gradually, sometimes painfully, but always beautifully and with great strangeness and unexpected excitement.

On September 17, 1966, came the fourth sinking of *The Curse*, which, at last, took the wind out of our sails and brought our extended folly for the Kenya Game Department to a dramatic close. We had the very last three crocs on board plus one Turkana croc-skinner and were returning from an all-night shoot on Shingle Island two miles offshore from Alia Bay when a storm came up unexpectedly and green waves began pouring over the narrow stern of *The Curse*, which was weighed down by the engine and the three crocs. We were about a half mile away from the safety of Shingle Island, going downwind in an increasingly high sea. It was more and more difficult keeping the waves out of the boat and impossible to turn back and face the windward power of the waves. Within minutes the situation became grave, bringing extra-real meaning to the saying "caught between the devil and the deep blue sea."

It was total PANIC STATIONS. Twelve hours of stalking was willingly wasted: our last three treasured crocodile specimens got heaved overboard. We were bailing madly and fighting to keep balanced in fast-building five-foot waves with deep and narrow turbulent troughs in between. It was like a tantalizing trapeze act in the looming sea. *Glug, glug—The Curse* took on more water than it could handle. We were down in the middle of nowhere, bobbing around like surprised corks in the wilderness. By luck the bow compartment trapped enough air to keep *The Curse* afloat for a few minutes, and that gave us valuable support while deciding what-to-do (Indian merchant's expletive).

Our major humanitarian problem was the skinner, nicknamed "the Wildman" as he spoke no Swahili or English—or anything we knew or understood. His life in dusty Turkanaland had not encouraged him to learn to swim. He held on grimly to the slowly sinking *Curse*, his normally carefree grin transformed into the unmistakable expression of a dead man—eyes wide and rolled back in shuddering heavenward glance.

With great difficulty, in the angry sea, Alistair disconnected our gas tank, the only thing on *The Curse* that floated. The next frantic minutes were spent emptying the high-octane avgas and giving swimming lessons to the grunting Wildman—basically the mad kicking of his feet while he clutched the tank. We sent him off in the direction of Shingle Island. His wits, suddenly sharpened by the occasion, did not fail him. The little red tank bobbed off into the crashing waves, more or less in the right direction . . . that a way.

By this time, for some reason, the aviation fuel from the emptied tank was stinging us badly. It dropped *down* through the water and burned us all over. There was little hope of doing anything about it. Alistair was the next to leave, swimming off grimly with his glasses on, hoping to reach the invisible island with his dismal eyesight.

I stayed behind to find my diary in the submerged hull. By luck, I had tied it up with some rough twine that was too long for the job and after three or four fruitless bang-about dives, groping amongst the ropes and bags and boxes of supplies swimming below in the metal cockpit, my

hand accidentally lucked into the frayed end of a piece of string. . . . It was my diary.

For years I'd been keeping journals, saving mixed-up scraps and clippings, dawdles and dipsy doodles, in daily diary layouts for the sheer pleasure of it, escapism: snapshots of buddies from school, snakes eating rats, rampaging rhinos, old photos worked on by the passage of time, bits of cloth, dry things, Captain Marvel and the Phantom, clippings from the Nairobi Standard, Picayune cigarettes, hog hairs, my hair, teeth and claws, run-over toads, fish scales, elephant tales, lizard tails, bits of bullets, bugs, twigs, seeds, plants, scorpion carcasses, snakeskin sheddings from lakeside lava rocks—all manner of minuscule jottings, scraps for a scrapbook—a homework assignment that nobody asked for. All glued down with Bostick and Patex (from Alibhai Sherif's on Kimathi Street) by the chronic scavenger. The pages would fill and fill and wrinkle in the gluing. It all meant nothing to anyone else but me, myself, and I.

But now, for the first time ever, it contained something irreplaceable: all of Alistair's croc data, markings, measurements, and tail-scale sequences. These were the first important entries ever. *Usefulness!* This gave me a thrill and made it all vital to save.

The next part is somewhat blurred in my mind: a long mile or so freshwater swim, clutching the fateful book, in a lake we discovered to have strong and dangerous currents, snakes, and giant fish—*not to mention 25,000 crocs*. Were they watching us now?

Sometime later Alistair enthusiastically told us how he went about drowning without actually minding:

> I soon ran into trouble. The waves took my glasses, and the water burned my eyes, leaving me unable to see . . . Eventually I started to panic. Unable to catch my breath, I felt a violent urge to thrash about, to struggle against fearful feelings. I had to force myself to keep control. Then I seemed to witness everything as an onlooker, detached and distant. Gradually my panic faded. I was by now very weak and numbed. The swimming continued but slowly and with great effort. I struggled to keep direction though I felt hopelessly lost. I felt that

drowning was a certainty. The fear of death was no longer an issue, for that seemed already decided. So I kept swimming, automatically, and for no better reason than there was nothing else to do. So when I saw the island's blurred shape—it had little reality for me until I sank down underwater and my feet actually touched bottom. I crawled along the bottom, slowly gaining an awareness of having reached some kind of ground. Then when I tried to pull myself up from the sea the breaking waves kept pushing me down and I nearly drowned again. I could see the Wildman, facing away from me, and tried to call him. But I made no sound, too worn out to even manage a whisper. Finally he turned and saw me in the wind and surf and ran to pull me out.

Alistair, with all his scientific training, meticulousness, accuracy, and objectivity, found himself confronted with a very shocking—or, just the opposite of a shock, most relaxing—*new set of feelings* in a circumstance hard to describe. It was drowning time and there was instead an all-encompassing ocean of calm, a reassuring new realm of reality—undeniably real—adding tranquillity, perspective, detachment, and distance to the anguish of a watery grave, particularly the panic of croaking, *final* moments, last gasps, the famous tunnel and the light—marvelousness—FANTASIA . . . It was a whole new world.

All the desperate days of struggle were gone:

- getting up
- going to work / school / recess / study hall / homework
- compulsory chapel / sacred studies / classical civilization / Latin, Greek, calculus, organic chemistry / *vacation*
- getting supplies, glasses, pills
- going to the bank, paying bills, doing repairs
- cleaning house, all chores
- DEBTS, illnesses, uphill battles, flat tires
- boring functions, Christmas presents, postcards from Pretoria, thank-you letters to relatives

- meetings, obligations, funerals, alimony
- toothpicks, toothpaste, dentists and doctors

all blended magically now into dreamtime serenity.

For several eerie, transitory moments, Alistair must have entered what has come to be known as the Holographic Universe, where he experienced a wait-and-see pudding: Surprise City! Altered states. Thrill of two lifetimes. How one deals with these moments of life-changing intensity obviously varies from person to person. We are trying to find answers but have a long way to go: the imagination and openness of youth compares favorably with the measurements and conclusions of most adults. And after all, *everything is relative.*

Sometimes, looking into the eyes of an old Turkana, I could feel for a moment, through the mechanical channels of the retina, a new frequency of access to haunting inner connectedness—like another dimension of understanding, as it used to hit me on the way to school when I saw my face reflected in the mail chute. Deep connectedness to something else—an all-knowing consciousness that turns the stomach—in the distance, way out in the subtler levels of reality, where this consciousness is already everywhere. Face to face at last with the fantastic nature of time and space . . . Einstein and beyond. After all, where *did* the consciousness of living things come from?

So Alistair found himself drowning and relaxing in a new dimension, scientifically pioneering the ambidextrous universe—the New Physics. He was not drowning so much as swimming back into his own mind—into the new world of thought-language and the vast collective unconscious, where, when you confront it, you know it. A near-death-experience researcher sums up the other levels of reality: "The spiritual core is so awesome and overwhelming that the person is at once and forever thrust into an entirely new model of being." All the earthly misconceptions are forgotten and forgiven in favor of compassion and understanding. So *that* was the point of life?

When I was about Zara's age, just starting school in the 1940s, the science teachers kept on saying how close we were to creating life in some laboratory. Now, half a century has gone by the tubes—and the closer scientists look the deeper the problem seems to have become. Quantum physics has magnified the mystery . . . somewhere we can't quite reach from such a conditioned and narrow dimension as ours as laid out at my school. It could be that somewhere behind the growing, reproducing cells is an infinitely vast ocean of energy and a weirdly endless circular shape to time and space. So far who can know—

The extended effort of staying alive in rough windswept waves was more than our muscles could stand. Without any salt in the water to hold us up we definitely had that sinking feeling. The current and the force of the waves worked at keeping us away from Shingle Island, a sandbank the length of a football field, now lying very low in the storm—barely visible from the top of a wave. My own arrival took quite a while, as I swam fighting the waves while clutching the clumsy 1966 diary.

I wasn't thinking about drowning yet, but having just lost binoculars, gun, camera, boat, and basically everything, I had many nightmarish thoughts swimming about in my bobbing bleary-eyed head. Where was the Wildman? Would the crocs be stirred up in this sea? A mile of waves and watery hopelessness, then at last the thin dark line of Shingle Island was up ahead—a perfect shelter for the many *mambas* (crocs) that lay there night and day, mouths open as if anticipating something fleshy. But none of this is what caught my attention . . .

"Always something new and strange out of Africa"—Pliny's famous truism entered my brain.

Two black silhouettes were running around in circles. Their arms were hugging and slapping and rubbing and shaking and throwing sand. One after the other dropped down, rolling and spinning—playing in the black sand, then into the sea, and back again—back and forth, up and down, in the water and out . . . slap, dash, hug, run, fall, rise. There was no sound track to this silent movie, just a foreground roar of crashing waves against the bluish-black sky of squall clouds.

I crawled up the beach like a drowned rat from the Omo River Delta, gasping and spluttering, but happy enough to emerge from the brownish sea of slime—dying to ask about the wild and crazy guys before my bloodshot eyes. *What* were they doing?

No one had to say a word. Heavy winds were blowing. Within a second the explanation came to me. Blustering breezes hit the burns of the avgas all over me. The difficulty of the swim had hidden this pain, but Rudolf's wind brought it back on Shingle Island. It was pure hell. If I'd only had a camera to record the loony dancing. We ended up with scabs all over. These scabs were the only proof of an otherwise inexplicable painful embarrassment . . .

But we were still facing the problem of getting off this wind- and wave-battered little prick of a tiny island.

Swimming with crocodiles is not as bad as they say if you have studied their stomach contents for several years and have confidence that lake crocs eat small fish (90% tilapia on Lake Rudolf) and leave the bigger Nile perch and human beings pretty much alone. But, of course, crocs, like other animals, love to prove humans wrong . . .

We waited until early afternoon, when the wind died down before changing direction, promising to make the two-mile swim to camp a lot easier. Standing in the murky shallows, joking about the odds

I feel it coming—I feel it coming—
Over my left shoulder, the primitive horror.

—T. S. ELIOT

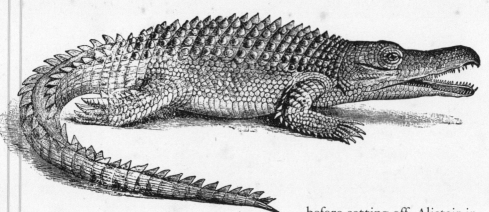

before setting off, Alistair in-quired: "Do you know what's yellow and treacherous?"

Answer: "Croc-infested custard."

So our pebbleworm survey was at an end. We were three crocs short of the "minimum biometric sampling" of crocodiles. Don't worry about what that means, it's just a scientific term for getting enough crocs to represent a large enough cross-section (of crocs) to spell out general truths about the whole population, the facts of their lives—these scaly, out-of-time, out-of-place "pebbleworms," Kroko-drilos—*Crocodylus niloticus.* Our study could very possibly determine their future, their potential usefulness and value, if anyone in the Game Department would read the report. For instance, crocs could be farmed instead of being shot on behalf of commercial fishermen, whose vast trawler nets cold-blooded crocs would swim though and destroy, once again making them "the enemy," "bad animals," inconvenient animals to which humans can then do whatever they want.

Just because wild animals such as crocs represent the savagery we mean to rise above does not mean that they have nothing else to offer the lonely soul of civilized man, so far removed from nature. Those who regret the thoughtless destruction of nature, who feel we are losing something irreplaceable, may have something real to tell us. As they say, "Look before you leap."

There are people who even *care* about crocodiles. They care because these beasts are part of the bigger systems of Nature, part of the fast-disappearing wild-deer-ness whose diversity and uniqueness not only spell survival, but can never be repeated. Such people hate to see that wildness and open freedom disappear before mankind has proved beyond a doubt that a full life can be enjoyed without it.

So the endless battle goes on: from "Karamoja" Bell and "Nyama Yangu" (Arthur Neumann) in the Northern Frontier District of Kenya, to Buffalo Bill in Cody, Wyoming, and the last great scouts, Geronimo and Sitting Bull at the Little Big Horn, Wounded Knee, or beyond. Man against Nature. Man against himself, tribalism, and territorialism . . . stress and density . . . bulldozers, cement, armaments (Defense Department), territorial conquest, loss of diversity, loss of time, loss of space, and time.

It was going to be a long swim home.

THE FATE OF THE

Reflections on Natural History / Lake Rudolf, Turco, Hug Reach & beyond

Paddling and kicking with the gas tanks, untold hours in the shifting winds, many miles of looking over the left shoulder in croc-infested waters, gulping and gurgling—a sort of last-gasp chiller called Terror of the Deep—we finally reached our old campsite on the eastern edge of Alia Bay.

We staggered ashore—happy to feel the slimy goo under our feet—pulling a make-do raft built with the Wildman's glorious gas tank and some tin containers that we'd ripped open to provide a kind of primitive sail. A jar of Skippy crunch-style peanut butter had been lashed onto the raft for emergency rations during the uncertain hours at sea. Skippy, Hellmann's, and Ritz crackers—we knew them well on this semidesolate safari. But now it was *shauri ya Mungu* (God's plan—said with a shrug of the shoulders). Our mission was over. I would pack up the camp while Alistair flew to Ferguson's Gulf. There he would organize a boat to come over and pluck the Wildman off Shingle Island where he was perched like a pelican, keeping his feathers dry, eager to retire from life on the high seas.

Waiting for us on shore against a background of vultures, ravens, and marabou storks—still fighting over last week's pile of dissected rotten-smelling carcasses—was our trusted cook, waving and pointing into the mud flats of our so-called front lawn.

In the expanse of dark mud that is typical of many bays on Lake Rudolf, at the far end of a stretch of sludge, was the unmistakable knobbly nut—the head—of a very old and wise-looking croc, complete with moss and barnacles, waiting . . . *"Well, I'll be a blue-nosed gopher . . ."*

He was no more than a stone's throw away, an unheard-of display of reptile insolence. How could this cheeky character possibly know that our long-drawn-out work program had just then come to a sinking end? *Na-kwisha kabisa*, as they say—"finished completely" during the blue-black squall. If so, had he become untouchable? What was his problem?

We had found out long ago that crocs are much more intelligent and far more complicated in all their behavior patterns than ever before estimated; but a large croc waiting for us in our own front yard was really weird.

Of all the big game, the ancient Kroko-drilos has the best combination of eyesight, hearing, and sense of smell.

At best it took us two hours for every daytime croc stalk. Any shift in the wind, any small sound, and it was *shauri kwisha*, the end of the scheme. Breaking the horizon, rising above it, with head or hand, or anything, meant the instant disappearance of all crocs around. The bigger the croc, the older and wiser it was.

Who could have thought that such a slap-in-the-face target would show up like this? And of course the twist of it was, we were unprepared, unequipped, uninterested, undone, and in fact quite ready to just pack up and leave. I was looking forward to a refreshing high-altitude holiday at Bill Woodley's Aberdare Rain Forest Park on the way home south toward Hog Ranch. Cool, quiet, forest photography with bushbucks, bongos, giant forest hogs, leopards, cape buffalo, eles, rivers of rain, rest and recuperation, at last back in Galo-Galo country, the famous Mau-Mau forest.

But this cold-blooded croc was quietly waiting out there in the primordial ooze. It was quite a puzzle trying to interpret what kind of message this was from friend or foe. At best it was a little haunting. At worst we might be *visited* at night. Who knew what was on his mind?

Only a month before, Alistair and I had experienced some amazing midnight croc aggression. It came from a twelve-footer we nearly didn't

get to measure. It came like a torpedo from more than thirty yards off-shore, barreling through the waves onto dry land, straight for the flash-light that I, unfortunately, was holding. Alistair was so taken by surprise, his two or three shots completely failed . . . and then, of course, the gun jammed. It wasn't the first time, but it could have been our last—hardly an ad for Winchester. *A charging croc*—from surf to turf? We'd never heard of anything like it! Once out of the water, it lunged forward with horrendous twisting leaps, wide-open jaws slam-ming shut like the rifle blasts we were not able to deliver. *BANG, BANG.* Nerve-shattering thunderclaps every few seconds, amazing motor-drive explosions of meat-eating carnivorous fury. Scared stiff, I held the flash-light out to the side and motored around in circles waiting for the finish-ing shots that did not come.

Alistair hurled his rifle to the ground, taking out his trusty Colt .45. I was really dancing now. At point-blank range he fired, again and again. The scaly leviathan was on autopilot with adrenaline overload, hell-bent for that flashlight and me. It took several loads to weigh this pebbleworm down with lead. This last dance was enough for me.

Usually, the big daytime crocs would take a whole afternoon to sight, stalk, prepare for a shot, and then possibly lose. So we carefully constructed camouflaged croc-blinds all over the lake, with secret path-ways worked out long in advance. Our expeditions in the burning sun,

crawling over broiling black lava rock or wriggling through spike grass, added great tension and heavy breathing when it came time to squeeze off a shot. At these times the pressure was really on. The whole job was agony, with disappointment looming at every squeeze-down.

Our Winchesters were aimed, sighted-in for targets one hundred yards away. We used silver-tipped .270 ammo for the straightest possible shot, but even when conditions were perfect—safely downwind to avoid the croc's keen sense of smell, with a solid rest for the gun, nerves calm—there were always plenty of screaming plovers or hissing Egypt-ian geese, relentless guard birds, hanging around, waiting to give us away. These feathered alarm systems were the most irritating side of togetherness—symbiosis at its worst. The life of many a croc over many hundreds of years has been saved by the piercing screams of its bird bud-dies. Undoubtedly more than once a busybody goose collected a bullet through an outstretched wing from an enraged hunter, a cloud of feath-ers erupting like a burst pillow. Then again, in camp at night the geese were very comforting standing guard for us in the same way.

Back at Alia Bay, we were still trying to figure out what kind of weirdo lay out there on our doorstep. A croc in waiting! What could it mean?

We were not superstitious in any way; after so long a time on the lake, the logic of the ages was fairly clear. But this sulking skulky freak intruder was getting under our skin . . . an old and worn-out pebble-worm knocking at our door.

So we unpacked loudly, laughed and swapped stories about the Wildman, noisy enough to irritate our newfound neighbor. We did every-thing but throw stones.

At times our strange visitor would move off. But then it would come back again as if our gooey lawn held some kind of secret attraction.

As peanut butter can go only so far, we urged Atagoigan, our cook, to take a *panga*, one of his long knives, to one of the submerged croc car-casses and chop us down a fresh feeding catfish to fry. This he did as if opening the icebox door to pull out a fillet. Catfish really love a good rot-ting croc carcass, and we loved them for loving it. Easy, fast, and delicious. As Atagoigan slashed his fish, the mysterious croc in the mud sank out of sight.

We were starving. The Hellmann's was ready. The fish was frying with the usual generous sprinkling of windblown sand. As the burning sun burned glorious red and sank behind the desert dunes, a distant Alia Bay lion gave out the kind of grunting you sometimes hear before a rain—but we knew *that* would never happen—not here anyway. *Bloop*— our visitor was back—same place, the same knobbly nut, black and barnacled, peering in our direction. He looked at us . . . we looked back at him.

Just before dark, Alistair flew off to organize a boat for the abandoned Wildman, still bedded down on his lonely island, far away, far gone, staring into space, no pillow in the black sand. My diary was out there with him, blowing in the wind. So there was nothing to do but pack things up and take a few last photographs of our carcass-covered campsite. Tomorrow, if all worked out, we would be gone for good. In the meantime, I had determined to take a crack at the ghostlike nutcase out front, if he was still with us in the morning. Curiosity was peaking. And we had one .270 rifle still in camp.

I couldn't help but think about the Olde English rhyme that long ago warned of weeping crocodyles lurking in yonder mud.

> As when a wearie traveller, that strayes
> By muddy shores of broad and flowing riversides . . .
> O'er perillous wandering wayes,
> Doth meete a cruell and craftie crocodyle,
> Which in false griefe, hyding his harmful guile,
> Doth weepe full sore, and sheddeth tender tears . . .
> The foolish man, that pities all the while
> His mournful plight, is swallowed up unawares
> Forgetfull of his owne, that mindes another's tears.

"Well, dearly beloved," as early wanderers would say to their attentive audiences at bedtime, I was never superstitious—but I never take chances either . . .

I felt all alone, and the darkest darkness of that final moonless windy night soon fell upon my lonely plight. Surrounded by rotting carcasses, the campsite was giving off most attractive smells for any meat-eating reptile—especially the old weirdo—so I moved my canvas camp bed into a more protected position between a hastily piled-up stack of equipment cases and the makeshift canvas wind-through shelter. Desert toads were squirming all around underneath the freshly moved metal cases—a viper's paradise but also a wall of protection . . . just in case. ZZZZzzzz. The howling wind that closed out all other sounds drove me into dreamland.

My last morning came peacefully. It was deep in purpley reds like the sunset and there was no wind at all. Nothing moved but the slightly lapping waves from all those weeks of wind and a fly or two that tickled my face, buzzed around, then landed again with sticky legs like melted butter. A *kikoi* cloth flapped over my face immediately for relief.

My skin was sore and scabbing up from yesterday's watery ordeal. Everywhere burned, including you-know-where. Tea. Ritz crackers. Pure Africa. Waiting for things to happen. Today . . . tomorrow . . . waiting happily: *shauri ya Mungu*. It's always God's plan.

Alistair was an excellent pilot. He liked moonlight landings and could bring a full load with ten or twelve crocs down just about anywhere—so long as the nose wheel didn't break through the earth's crust and dig into soft sand, sometimes requiring a day or two of digging out. But who could say when he would return?

No diary to write in. No dissections to perform. No . . . *Wait a minute!* I peered out onto the soggy mud flats. A family of Egyptian geese were feeding in the reeds. Skimmer birds were skimming the shallows. Marabou storks were poised like patient undertakers mourning for the dead. And there, center stage, was the mystery mugger, his crusty old cranium pointed at me exactly as it had yesterday. Motionless, ancient, ageless, steadily staring, the croc of all time, demanding investigation. Maybe it was nuts?

I was up for it. There was nothing but time. I loaded up rifle number 2 . . .

Long ago we had invented a water-stalk technique for desperate daytime maneuvers when it was too hot for stalking on dry land. With the loaded gun, on its open vinyl case, resting on a floating inner tube, Alistair would drop me over the side at a suitable distance from a beach of basking crocs. The boat would go and I would drift in, slowly, head hidden, up against the tube . . . slowly, slowly to the shore. Floating onto solid beach . . . sand washing into pants filling the pockets anchoring me into the equatorial landscape. Steady the gun, click off the safety . . . fire at the biggest, smartest, most difficult pebbleworm—sometimes between the open jaws of a basking companion, sometimes getting chased away. Some muggers are territorial.

So now I grabbed the black inner tube and slipped into the murky mud.

Uhhhhh shhlushleeee uhhhhhhh. Already this was a very different experience. This was heavy-duty ooze—a beauty treatment at Elizabeth Arden, or a Baden-Baden mud pack. It felt divine. This goo was *to die for.* This would keep me young forever.

I gunked a glob of the glamorous goo onto my neck and shoul-

ders . . . camouflage . . . health cream (possibly part pelican poo). I slid along the shore as never before . . . another handful into the hair, rub it into scalp with fingertips like this . . . forehead smeared . . . utterly divine! A treat instead of a treatment. Gliding through with slimy cheek pressed against the warm black rubber tube. This was something else.

Never daring to peek ahead. A cool current in the deeper mud—then warm again. Tilapia swimming and feeding in the reeds. No one cared, although a flabbergasted goose stared a little. I could do this swim all day. Months on Alia Bay and we'd never tried this before . . . what fools! I went slower and slower in a kind of wallowing ecstasy like a delirious hippo. The animal I'd always wanted to be. No one was within a million miles of my mental mood. I paused and waited. I felt like Nguya. I was in his head. A frozen dark statue. The hunter and the hunted. Undetectable, unnoticeable, unseen, mud-caked movements. At one with the wet earth, I lay there in my sea of slime.

The sun beat down and baked my mud-caked head and neck. The mud cracked, the water slapped, the cool came back. I slithered and seeped into the soupy slop. Gravity was gone. I was a frog. My popping eyes peeked out over the swamp. I was evolution. Dark Ages. Going back . . . I wasn't me. I was a glop of gluey swamp, cooling, cracking, crawling for the croc.

A breeze was coming up. It mattered not, encased as I was in layers of crusty protection. I sunk into hidden pathways of pleasure and purest muck. The wind got up, its quiet gentle direction, head on, perfection. From clump to clump, I eased my rump. The slowest creature in a pre-historic play. Encased, in ecstasy, invisible to any other being.

I eased the gun-case cover back and raised my mud head. Reeds around me. A bug, a bird. A softest-of-breezes, my grimy paw slipped over an eight-power scope. A window to another world. Periscope up. My beady eye got the view. Two degrees right. I weighed onto the tube. Slightly solid slimeways . . . a caked sunbaked bit of hair blowing in the moving air. Reeds bending. Little waves lapped over. Motionless again.

I saw him seeing me, seeing him, seeing me. Great big moist eyes without expression, "pitiless as the sun," vertical pupils of the great dragon. *Blink*. A magic membrane pulls across the clearest lens. The magnification of the moment. Hugeness. Scaliness. Ancientness. Encrustedness. Clearest eyeballs locked in place. Armor, mud, me, it. *Blink*. Dragonflies appear, hover, fixed in the wind. The whole scene is a museum window—a diorama for real.

He doesn't move. Black cranium. Mossy mugger—barnacles and bugs in a floating witches' garden. Glare stare nostrils flare, mankind beware. Ease the safety off. *Click*. Silver-tipped explosive . . . *the darkness that may be felt?*

A swamp, a sea. Assignment, alignment. Confinement. Biology, zoology. Zoos, choose, lose. Aim between his eyes. Imagine 170,000,000 years. *Blink*. Sigh. Sun. Cry. Run. Die. Why? Captain Bligh. Goodbye, guy.

You think of these crazy rhymes sometimes when you squeeze down, because it takes your mind off the job and you don't flinch in anticipation of the shot.

The oncoming drone of Alistair's airplane broke the magic of the moment. From Ferguson's Gulf to Shingle Island and here—Wildlife Services emergency rescue service! Check the sight . . . I flicked the safety back into place . . . muttered "Bango." The great splash and frantic croc escape were all seen and much appreciated from up above.

The Happy Mud Man staggered ashore and went to greet the plane. In minutes my second skin dried, baked hard. *Pottery Man was born* and liked his new role so much he decided to spend the whole day that way.

The old croc settled in his ooze, took his long-awaited snooze.

THE TRUTH COMES THROUGH THE STRANGEST DOOR

Lunch

Evening

When the Wildman was rescued and transported to Alia Bay and handed Pottery Man back his diary, there was a rush to see if the baby-croc-measurements section had escaped unharmed from the dreaded depths. It was there, readable, lists in ballpoint pen intact, the survey records saved. In fact, everything was there—the whole diary. Every waterlogged page had been turned, over and over for all those hours on windy Shingle Island, the work of the Wildman. Each soggy diary day had been kept apart from the next with bits and pieces of this and that; strands of seaweed, bones, and Shingly sand got fitted in between the pages. Methodically, systematically, in my friend's calloused wood-hard hands, all was separated and dried with great care and saved. Great soaking stains sank through the parchment pages. Running ink and drooling goo were frozen in those Rorschach blobs we used to make at school. I creased myself with laughter when I saw it. I was wrong to laugh.

It was a gift from the gods: the ink-embedded photos never looked so good. Without plan or design, they came to light on stormy isolated Alia Bay; nine months of hoarded scraps had fossilized themselves together. Before my eyes the unrelated pieces merged in monstrous mildewed unities of trivial pursuit, bursting forth in clouds of spill and drip, great blossoms exploding in the wind. Soaked-through seepings turned from mess to magic. The wondrous workings of pure chance! Jottings and clippings bonded underwater, falling swimmingly into place. All my photos peeled and dyed, dried differently from anything I could have dreamed: bleached out on top, fermenting underneath, all nice and rotten, runny and dry. A liquid tapestry bled to the edge. I seemed to be seeing those ruined pictures for the very first time. The scales fell from my eyes.

Engawaa, ni furaha nyingi (I'm really happy)—and I really was. *Asante sana kweli. Kazi yakn safi kabisa na maradadi, mzuri* (Thank you truly, you did a beautiful job), I said over and over to my wild Turkana friend, who understood nothing of these words, but who knew I cared. He must have squatted there for hours on end, day and night, turning those 365 soggy days, letting each one dry little by little. He had quietly created something from nothing and given new meaning to Einstein's belief that imagination is more important than knowledge.

The Wildman had done me one of the greatest favors of my life. He handed over 1966, painted, with drip-dry inky layers of fresh ideas, veiled, overlaid, overlapped, stained, scarred, scratched, etched, branded, shot through with raw truth. The diary year was watercolored, weather-beaten, wonder-ridden, spontaneously spilled, and sensorially saturated in wild collage. It looked like a swollen carcass, tied up with string. But it worked. It was chaos in order, a magician's soup, a sea of images. There were rips and warps and see-through sections, soaked and dried and unified, each page a wave, all the same and all different. Each one was new, yet old, beyond intent, flowing in harmony. It was unfathomable contentment in ruination, with birth and death on every page.

Pottery Man, dried and cracked, held an offering from the sea, lessons never learned at school. He found it life enhancing. It changed his point of view. The truth comes through the strangest door. Here was a fresh look at an ugly accident, a new way to see the tragedies and triumphs lying ahead. "All is for the best in the best of all possible worlds" (Dr. Pangloss). Whatever it was, I was hooked. The joyful surprise had helped to show where beauty lies.

> Full fathom five thy father lies,
> Of his bones are coral made;
> Those are pearls that were his eyes:
> Nothing of him that doth fade,
> But doth suffer a sea-change,
> Into something rich and strange.
> —SHAKESPEARE, *The Tempest*

UNDER THE MISTS OF
THE KENYA SNOW

Aberdare National Park warden Bill Woodley was enthusiastic, involved, experienced, friendly, interested in photography, and open to new ideas. His years of national service during the Kikuyu Revolution against British rule, historically known as the Mau-Mau Emergency, put him in touch with all the top-ranking, hard-core Mau-Mau generals—cunning survivors of a guerrilla war that lasted four years in the forest, fighting the British army, the King's African Rifles, the Kenya police, and pseudo-gangs of local Kenyans (including Woodley) who blackened their faces, carried homemade guns, wore bush rags for clothes, and made daring contact with the enemy through captured informers.

Bill Woodley

All this would help him when independence came to Kenya in the early 1960s. Warden Woodley (nicknamed "Wildlife William" in the newspapers) needed first-rate talent for his jungle park. No one could outdo the top ten generals of the Wa-Kikuyu terrorist army, so Wildlife William signed them all on.

Their employment was controversial to say the least, but these bush wizards performed brilliantly under Woodley and, until the day he left, his park never even began to suffer the tragic fate of being poached out.

There is another reason why Bill Woodley would become the most successful of game wardens in Africa. More important than anything else, he brainstormed, designed, and built a covered ditch and fence that prevented elephants, buffalos, and rhinos from leaving their isolated national park island of "protection." He had devised a way to interrupt their age-old urge to migrate from small crowded places and their boundless joy in stomping on the forbidden cornfields, tea and coffee plantations, cattle and pigs just outside the park. *And why not, after all, who was here first?* The now-famous Woodley ditch was revolutionary then, a key to future park management. It was all hand-dug and double-fenced for more than forty miles, separating the wildlife and the pigs.

Wildlife William allowed me to build a small house in the middle of his great Aberdare rain forest. It was to be a blind, a bivouac bedroom, a diary-studio hideaway. And the original idea behind it was to photograph his animals and publish the results, to teach his rangers how to do the same, to demonstrate how photography can best utilize big game to create books and magazine articles—general education, visual messages from the haunts of Nature—and a greater reality than our own.

So it wasn't long before I was living in the high-altitude equatorial forest in a Robinson Crusoe cedar-barked shack, in the middle of paradise. It was a garden on the equator full of elephant, buffalo, leopards, lion, and rhino, and, most important and never photographed before in its wild kingdom, the ultraelusive bongo, a 700 lb streak of striped lightning—mostly reddish-brown in color, with outsized ears, long menacing horns, great wet see-through eyes, hyperactive nose, and smooth flowing catlike moves if anyone ever sees one. You can shoot bongos through the thick bamboo with heavy rifles, but to get close enough to take a clear shot with a camera is by far the greater game. One assistant warden, Charles Moore of the Aberdare Park Service, left after a dozen years never having seen a bongo.

The first thing that had to happen was the construction of my 20-by-10-foot cedar off-cut hut. Peter Wanjohe was the National Park *fundi* (expert carpenter), and within a matter of days his crew had the whole delightful structure standing up, half nailed together, right next to the Ian Player white rhino pens. Every plank, with rough bark outside, was carefully numbered and would get its nails pulled out and then be carried six miles into the Ruhuti River Valley for reconstruction. Wanjohe positioned the hut like a bridge over a dripping waterfall. We hoped the sound of falling water would hide accidental noises, conversation, hiccups, Ritz cracker chewing. Compared to Lake Rudolf, the scene was perfect, idyllic, sandless, windless, wonderful. I had one door and one window overlooking a natural salt lick on a slightly banked island with the Ruhuti gently flowing by on either side. In the heat of midday this

stream was just deep enough for me to sink six inches underwater into a bed of watercress and have a deeply satisfying soak before lunch—watercress sandwiches slathered with Hellmann's. In a Garden of Eden jungle paradise.

Some evenings a bushbuck couple would come to the small island nestled in the protection of the waterflow rippling by. They would lie there like sculptures close to each other, chewing their cud, staring into the darkening bush, waiting for nighttime.

But I was waiting for bongos, the probable distant relatives of the bushbuck with their massiveness of body and curving horns. But they also called to mind the giant eland.

President Roosevelt's historic safari in 1909 secured the first photos of a bongo trophy (above), collected for him by his hunter Philip Percival. My hope was to capture one on film alive. But we knew it would be a long ordeal—like maybe never.

Plate 20

The Striped Antelope
Published by Thos Kelly Paternoster Row 1817

The elusive bongo

Waiting for Bongo

When the hut was first put up I spent two very quiet and very relaxing recuperative diary-clipping weeks escaping from the desert winds of Rudolf with Mau-Mau generals at watch by the waterfall. Hyrax choruses kept us company at night—also two small mice named Hoppington and Hoppington Jr., who loved nibbling along with us at mealtime. Especially when Skippy chunky-style peanut butter was served.

As diary time passed by, a whole new photographic strategy was conceived for the bongo hunt. Sitting around waiting was productive for clipping and gluing but not for photographing *nyama* (wildlife).

It was decided that Galo-Galo Guyu, General Chui, General Kifaru, and park sergeant Kamau (head ranger) would all be required to help attain our ultimate goal. With their extra help we would be able to cover the Ruhuti area, up and down both ridges, all the way to the bamboo and beyond, including the frosty moorlands at an altitude of over 10,000 feet. It would be a hit-or-miss operation, bashing through the *bundu* (the bush), swift and ongoing, but a rich visual catch was assured. Throughout the 1950s, '60s, and '70s the Aberdares were in fact the most densely crowded wildlife area in the world.

So Galo-Galo journeyed up from Hog Ranch, where he'd been busy replanting Mbagathi Forest seedlings around my tents, landscaping the Ranch, including some magic *muguma* trees, the sacred tree of the Masai and the Kikuyu tribes—the tree where warriors pray.

Warden Woodley hadn't seen Galo-Galo for quite a while, so we enjoyed an old-style upcountry *wompo-bash* (drinks party) at the dilapidated Mweiga *matatu* Mini Bus Taxis stop. One quick shopping trip at Osman Allu's all-purpose *duka* (provisions store) in the nearby town of Nyeri and we were away. After so many months of Lake Rudolf moonscape, Mwiega was like stepping out of a time capsule onto the other end of another world. Kenya can do that for you. One day you're drowning with crocodiles in a desert lake and the next you're in a rain forest, half frozen, pursuing *Ndonguru*, the ultraelusive supersensitive bongo.

It was a long six-mile walk to our new Ruhuti River camp. In the manner of the early foot safaris, about a dozen rangers came along with camp beds, sleeping bags, weeks of food, lots of big lenses, diary supplies, and high-speed Tri-X film.

Steep hills, narrow trails, scurrying giant forest hogs, Cape buffalo encounters face to face at every corner, constant elephant rumblings vibrating up and down the gurgling riverbanks. Throughout the 1950s and '60s the Aberdare Rain Forest elephants were violent and unpredictable as a result of white man's military harassment. All the Mau-Mau hideouts and hot spots in the forest were full of gaping bomb craters. Elephants don't forget things easily and for many years those blasted bombs caused some very weird and threatening elephant behavior.

Colobus monkeys flew from tree to tree, flashes of black-and-white fur, keeping an eye out for the big predator eagles, which could swoop down the valley in seconds and grab them. Guilty-headed hyenas shuffled away into the underbrush. Red forest duikers, rarely seen miniature deer, posed delicately before vanishing with a whistle of pure panic, bulging black eyes frozen in fear, urgent little noses twitching, then gone. For some of these creatures survival was a totally terrorizing full-time occupation. It makes you think.

The Red Forest Duiker, hidden away (at dead center) GONE in 1/125th of a second—

Eventually we reached our waterfall shack in jungly drizzle, cool and wet, unloaded our packs, and settled in.

Stumpy

There was an old forest rhino that lived within a half mile of our new blind. He was in bad condition, with some deep infections in his front legs. He could not move easily or very far. His horn must have been very long once, but now it was broken off near the base, earning him our nickname: "Stumpy." From his hard life of injury and immobility he was a short-tempered rhino. He often offered us a convenient warm-up service, photography practice, in the early mornings or whenever you wanted to start off a new film—Stumpy was always nearby. *Click*—rush and stumble—*click click*—Heavy Drama! "*Every time a coconut.*" When in a long-drawn-out pursuit of bongo, all diversions are welcome and recommended. Stumpy was an essential side-attraction in our long ordeal.

After the Darajani-Randall rhino training school, beating down the bush in trucks, Stumpy was a piece of cake. He was hypersensitive and could hear us coming from across the valley. He would brace himself

"Stumpy" at the ready

when we got focused in at an easy range—no problem—but one *click* and Stumpy would leap forward as far as his hind legs could propel him. *Click* again—*Snort! Crash!* A ten-foot jump-charge of adrenaline to warm up the day.

I heard months later that the Kenya Capture Committee had been informed about Stumpy and had come to get him. After repeated misses with costly dart guns at huge unnecessary distances—fifty yards or more—they finally delivered an overdose of their M99 tranquilizer right into his ribs and watched poor Stumpy drop . . . never to rise again. He breathed his last, asleep in rhino dreamland. It was always hard to avoid this "Capture" Committee, although everybody tried.

Sergeant Kamau and I did the first photo reconnaissance walks up and down the Ruhuti River Valley, leaving Kariuki (General Kifaru) and Ndirangu (General Chui) to explore their old haunts and Mau-Mau hideouts. Galo-Galo stayed behind to unpack and to organize the blind, decorating it with all his bushcraft and artwork. There was no schedule or any hurry at all to our random photographic travels. This was our approach—skattergun indirect. One way or the other, each day we had some kind of fantastic photographic fortune. From large groups of grunting swine to poachers with dogs, from world-record rhinos to the biggest buffalos in Africa, from long-haired silver-colored lions on the freezing moorlands to midnight black leopards and spotted cerval cats, from colobus monkey–eating eagles to ill-tempered man-hunting elephants! And exotic secretary birds—long legged, oriental in appearance, fond of poisonous snakes. So many animals, our cameras were busy, you almost couldn't miss. But nowhere . . . Bongo.

An Eighty-Foot Fall

One day, when we hadn't even gone very far, Sergeant Kamau froze in his tracks. In the far distance was the unmistakable sound of a really furious battle between some huge enemies. Monstrous roaring shook the forest. We ran forward in this direction following game trails, minute after endless minute, chasing the fight between giant ventriloquists throwing their enraged voices across river valleys. The farther we went, the farther ahead the sounds seemed to be. Run. Stop. Listen. Run. Stop. Listen. Roaring, snarling, growling, exploding echoes of entanglement shook the woods. *Somewhere* humongous protestations were taking place.

"*Shauri ya chui*" (leopard problem), Kamau stated matter-of-factly. With an excited roll of his eyeballs he sprang forward, correcting our approach by a new series of paths closer to the river. Then across it, over and up, water gushing into my boots, each of us clamoring up a steep vertical bank of nettles, across a small open glade, and into

a giant Cedar forest. *RRRRoarrr GNAASHAHRRRRR* shook the trees. Kamau was racing from trunk to clump, stump, mound, bush—straining to see. My camera was all set. We just couldn't seem to get there. Racing forward with mercury moves, Kamau finally stopped, crouched low, and

pointed ahead. I dropped by his side, desperate to feast my eyes on what
had to be the battle of the century.

I saw a few milliseconds of the most highly concentrated somer-
saulting blurs of frantic air-clawing. Then, in the very miracle of the
whole shocking struggle, the bottom section of this whirling ball of fury,
all spinning and twisting, coughed up a spine-chilling grunt and scrab-
bled up the nearest, highest cedar tree, up, up into its uppermost
branches, probably eighty feet above us. All in seconds, as its opponent,
less wounded, streaked off into thick bush. There had been no time for a
single shot of this monster leopard fight. How we had been spotted,
smelled, or in any way detected in the middle of that savage battle was
astounding. One huge *chui* was up a tree, and photographing any leopard

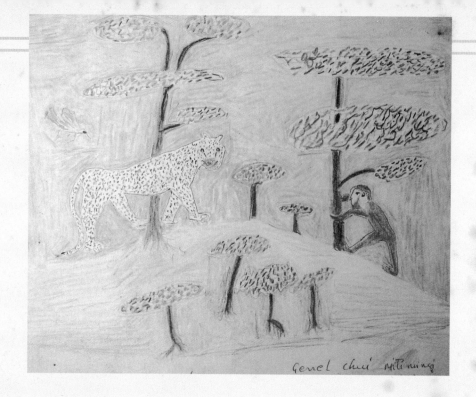

Genel chui mitimingi

while out on foot was very unusual and desirable. The tree was directly in front of us. Urgently searching the upper branches for movement, I pressed forward. *"Yeye naona wewe."* (He's looking at you.) Kamau had him spotted. Peering through the telephoto lens, I saw him blending into the pattern of the leaves, a perfect mix. I took a step nearer. He changed his branch, one leg half dangling, torn at the shoulder. *Click.*

He was the clear loser in whatever round of the fight we'd interrupted. I had him in perfect focus and was getting in closer. *Click.* New position. *Crack. Scuffle. Slip.* A whirring whistling noise hurtling through the air, rushing down, nearly on top of me, from maximum tree height. The leopard loser fell out of his tree.

I just hunched there in place. Here it was, all coming down . . . the final payoff that everyone felt I always deserved . . . *Thud!* Right next to me. (Missed by ten feet!) But shook the forest floor and everything around me . . . bounced way up in the air, bounced at least as high as my head. My eyes took in every detail—motor-drive high-speed vision at eye level. I followed it all. Here was force and flexibility. A miracle of muscles. From the height of the bounce, having landed on his back in an explosive impact of twisting flexible steel and rubber feline joints, the leopard squirmed around right side up to land on his feet, facing me.

Eye to eye for a fraction of a second.

Then he exploded off on three good legs, apparently unfazed by a drop of eighty feet.

Cape Buffalo

This is a Cape buffalo I shot (with film) while searching for our bongo in the Ruhuti River Valley. Of all the millions of buffalo ever hunted for world-record-class trophies, this one here, less than one mile from my waterfall blind, is the biggest and the best. Who needs more?

Cape buffalo are supposed to be the most dangerous of all the big game, but after running into untold thousands of them over the years, I would have to speak up in favor of their character. Retiring, reticent, shy, mind-your-own-business, always willing to back down, they are certainly not "the most dangerous game," as hunters claim. I can only guess their fearsome reputation comes from ones that hunters wounded. Even if nicked in the foot, they soon lie down, and, of course, the trackers come across them *mara moja*, stumble right onto them in thick bush, and so it seems as if the cunning brutes have ambushed them, staged a sneak attack. Except for occasional bachelor bulls, old and ill-tempered, these majestic animals are anxious to avoid humans, and when not unduly

pressed they provide magnificent sculptural power that seems to sum up the best of African wildlife.

Here is a world-record-class rhino found at high altitude, almost on the moorlands at about nine thousand feet. I think it's a female but never had time to check. The whole experience took less than a minute. The rhino came out into the open. *Click. Click.* "She" got quite upset and then retreated back to bush without any sign of aggression. Rhino reactions to danger usually consist of a loud snorting, blundering, heavy breathing, semiblind assault, a crude animalistic strategy that worked for centuries until some cunning mortal invented that magic dust called gunpowder. Such rhino behavior is so old-fashioned, so predictable, that avoidance is easy and to get skewered by a rhino requires a lot of very bad luck.

Forest Elephants

The Aberdare elephants best represent the big game. One-tuskers—or worse, no-tuskers—fully demonstrate their extreme sensitivity and near-human complexity. If they are really upset, injured or impaired, or manically disgruntled after years of bombs exploding in their territory—or all of the above—they *will* get you in one way or another. This has been proved by the game warden of the Northern Frontier (Rodney Elliott), who fanatically tracked-up and investigated every rogue attack in his area. The elephants always got their man, no matter what. But this extreme behavior is very rare, and it takes a lot of trying to get a real elephant charge: silent, head down, tusks scraping the ground—terrifying! Dusty "demos" are what most intruders witness. The elephant whirls around and faces you, head up, ears forward, with a towering body seemingly inflated to enormous size—you feel tiny and dangerously exposed. Elephant demonstrations can include such spectacular displays as tearing branches off trees and throwing them in your direction. Several elephant hunters have recorded instances where humans were literally buried by this extrovert technique. Once a blind woman had to be rescued from under a mountain of thorny debris that was heaped upon her by a very angry ele.

Between 1967 and 1972, I filled the cedar-plank walls of my home-from-home bivouac-blind with daily lists of animals and incidents. The whole interior became a sort of Robinson Crusoe diary on wood. Through rain, sleet, heavy mist, and glorious sunshine, and sometimes all four in one day, I recorded every single thing. Ever since the Wildman gave me the hand-dried croc diary, fresh from its watery grave, a real Rudolf reincarnation, I had become a daily-diary nut, a slave to trivia and all manner of petty diversions—diversifications all over the walls (I'm sure it's all still there) and in my Letts Standard Nairobi Diary. I got it all down with Bostik, Pattex, and Uhu to ferment and decay and even burn over the years to come. List after list, I loved it all as I waited contentedly for a shot at the great bongo, more elusive than I had ever expected. But it was more fun taking it slowly, living spontaneously from surprise to surprise. Africa taught this, as in: *shauri ya Mungu.*

squabbling
elephant
aberdare
forest
near
maragat?
1972
for the End
of the game
Peter Beard

Hog Ranch
By Artist Mwangi
Feb. 1998

Hog Ranch
by Mwangi Kuoi
Feb 1998

Daily Surprises

There was the day a colobus got in between me and my outhouse (bush). A monkey standoff with menacing fangs, grunting clucking outbursts sounding like knuckles down a washboard, standing upright and jumping about like an agitated human. No chance to do *anything* . . . long minute to slowly edge backward.

Or the two full days spent freeing a rhino that had slipped accidentally into Wildlife William's deep-down ditch in a particularly wet and muddy section—untold hours of digging and pulling, coaxing and cajoling the mud-caked monster who eventually, on release, snorted us up trees and kept us up there for quite a long time.

Or finding a forest rhino adopted by a herd of buffalo, staying right there in amongst them. They seemed to need one another and were quite at ease.

Or the night General Kifaru fell off the food shelf, where he often slept—a drop of about six feet. Galo-Galo interpreted the crash as a nocturnal raid and sprang into defensive action, crocodile *panga* at the ready.

Or the day we climbed up to the highest-altitude hideout of Field Marshal Dedan Kimathi, the Kikuyu's Mau-Mau god, and saw a male colobus beat off an attacking eagle with ferocious squeals and screams.

Or the day Sergeant Kamau and I watched an angry elephant across the Muringata River Valley tracking us by sense of smell with its outstretched trunk reading our progress on the ground, furious—and catching up to us as well!

Or all the various leopard sightings, or listening to elephants crashing through the bamboo. Or the sleeping ele on its side, sleeping against a steep bank, snoring loudly. We left him there unaware of our little visit.

Or the sad day we got back and found Hoppington Jr. drowned in an open jar of Skippy. The top was accidentally left half off and he had gone down into the delicious chunky-style goo.

Or my day on the Ruhuti with Veruschka, the six-foot-tall *Vogue* model, spotting a bongo bull in the distance, only minutes after the luckless assistant warden had dropped us off and left.

Or our three encounters with Kikuyu bongo poachers with their African hunting dogs racing through the bamboo.

Or the many spectacular days we watched the peaks of snowcapped Mount Kenya emerge from swirling storm clouds—*under the mists of the Kenya snow.* Irresistible photographs.

Or the drizzling evening when a gross and smelly spotted hyena freaked out of his bug-eyed head after accidentally walking into our blind. Turning around, I saw him looking into my face from about three feet away. Bulging eyes . . . jumping out of his skin.

From Bushbuck to Bongo

But of all the thrills and spills, diary day after diary day, the greatest wildlife moment of my thirty-six years in Africa finally came as I hoped it eventually would, one misty afternoon with Galo-Galo in panting pursuit of an open-daylight photo opportunity of a whole group of magnificent earth-red, finely striped trophy bongos.

As the years had ticked by, several times we had managed to capture bongo legs, side stripes, and rear ends *on film*. We even got in amongst the bongos, large herds of them. But I only got bits and pieces on film.

Bongos crave very thick bush and in the Aberdares the wind is always tricky. Approaches are frustrating—from thick to thicker—maddening. Stalk time is very limited in the steep valleys and on the hillsides—careful slow stalks are ruined because the wind turns around on itself and gives your scent away. We always had to carry a sock with ash inside to continually test the exact direction of whatever breeze there was. We also noticed that walking in the rain is a good idea because it seems to settle the animals down—they tend to come out of the dripping bush a bit. On a rainy day you could come around a corner and just about trip over a giant forest hog standing there, semi-gāgā, right in the way.

It was on just such a low-light drizzling day that Galo-Galo and I were tripping along a game trail on an open ridge. Just over the rim, conveniently blocked by a fallen tree, was a delicately poised male bushbuck, unaware of our passing. Although quite common, this quiet creature is one of the most photogenic in the forest, a sleek ghost that glides through thick foliage with the hunching harmonious grace of a cat, soft and delicate beyond words, moist, wild, flawless, pure magic, in all its movements a direct product of God.

Here was a poetic-photo opportunity, so Galo-Galo and I eased into perfect positions against the accommodating half-dead fallen tree. All circumstances were ideal. We were undetected. Both cameras were loaded, exposures correctly set. A light rain hushed the drama. During

many months and years of sharing photo experiences with Galo-Galo Guyo and the Mau-Mau generals, much time was spent gradually preparing them to operate spare cameras on their own, for their own regular patrols . . . Photography—an unutilized resource. But focusing was the one problem. Here was a chance to check it out and get it right. We were virtually invisible, side by side, with perfect rests for the telephoto lenses. Galo-Galo went first, arduously focusing, heavily pressing his camera rest into the fork of a thick branch. *Click*. Pass it over to me. I looked through the viewfinder, focused it my way, then passed it back to him. *Kali kabisa* (totally sharp). *Click*. More focusing, *click*. Pass it back for refocusing. The buck was quietly jumping out of his skin. *Snort*. Ears searching for some hint of identification, it took a brave catlike step in our direction—major puzzlement! We bracketed the lens openings, as light was low. Galo-Galo jammed the camera into the completely solid, vibration-free rest of the tree and with determined focusing and plenty of time, clicked it off . . . eased it over to me . . . inevitable refocus, even whispering hints of encouragement, slowing down the speed of exposure . . . *click* . . . passed it over again, and again. Eventually this became humorous, we were practically talking—all three of us at home with one another. It was delightful. It was too good to be true.

Right now the subject was immaculate, wildly cooperative, absolutely puzzled, rigid with curiosity, but at one with all the elements in its rainy jungle world. For a moment even the sun came out.

Within four or five minutes outbursts of wild satisfaction could be plainly heard from our area: all speeds and openings had been tried with horizontal and vertical framing, all had been achieved. Immensely self-satisfied, we crept away, leaving the poetic creature to strain and blink without us. It was a stunning achievement.

We quickened our pace. The afternoon was passing. I kept the longer and heavier lens, Galo-Galo had the other, the one containing what we were convinced were the best forest photos to date. Time passed. We crossed ridges. The drizzle was very fine in the air now, delicately drifting clouds of mist stretched through the valleys. This was the Aberdares at its lyrical best.

We meandered over a rise, and as we headed down a narrow game trail for some darker forest, I glanced back for a second, in the way that one sometimes does for no known reason at all, and directly saw a group of large reddish-brown forms all in a formation, right out in the middle of an open glade on an opposite ridge about two hundred yards behind us. In the great wet rich green silence of the rain, their startling red coats almost vibrated off the luscious emerald background. There was no hint that they were aware of our passing. Four female bongos right out in the open after so many months of trudging—this at last was the fabled *ndonguru* available for a full telephoto portrait.

Like the Nandi Bear in the Mau, or the Abominable Snowman of the Himalayas or Bhutan, like Big Foot in the High Sierra, this was the huge and delicate mystery beast that so few palefaces had ever seen alive. Here it was, the reason we had been walking twenty miles a day for all these months, in fact for several years now. There were the long horns spiraling up overhead, with piercing white ivory tips; huge nervously cupped hairy ears like supersensory antennae to pick up any foreign vibration or sound at any distance; a dozen or more stripes on either side of the body, particularly effective camouflage in the bamboo. The weight of a full-grown bull is 700 lbs or more!

Galo-Galo was retreating back to find me as I checked the light and got my heavy-duty 500 mm Russian lens poised for some quick insurance shots before running in. We hoped the rest of this herd was lurking behind, males and females hidden in the thick stuff. We felt optimistic. Resting the long lens on Galo-Galo's left shoulder, lens wide open in the low light, shutter speed at 1/250 of a second, I impatiently squeezed off five or six shots. Then we ran. Even in fine drizzle, whatever movement of air there is, it can't be trusted not to give ugly human scent away. Flushed with the confidence of our last exercise, hungry for the impossible, silently we tore down the steepest deepest paths cutting right to the valley floor, our final approach route to the right-hand side of the glade halfway up the opposite slope.

Urgent minutes of utmost rush. Galo-Galo was ahead, always knowing every best move, anticipating every turn, every bush, choosing the perfect route in stalking—as in life itself. He was the hunter and the prey, so easily could he sense the other, and touch the harmony of the exchange. He knew it all. Barefoot, wet, gliding down, bent over double without a sound, we were trying for a record on this one.

Breathing hard at the fifty-foot mark, we exchanged cameras quickly and I went into the last desperate stretch on hands and knees with Galo-Galo's close-up bushbuck camera. Rainy dampness helped greatly . . . nothing scraped or snapped . . . one knee after the other . . . totally down and out of sight, inching forward. A clump of twisted tree wreckage, already spotted and considered from across the way, offered complete cover and a direct view of the glade. This was my goal.

It was on the downhill end where the forward-most bongo was last seen grazing out in front. All very close now. Ten yards to go, not a sound in the forest. A drip or two of misty rain. I checked the camera over and over. Distance okay, film wound and ready, speed knob set in place at $\frac{1}{250}$ of a second. I mentally projected the strain of the bongos. Surely they knew something was happening—their X-ray vision telescoping through the branches, all their radar out. We would have to be geniuses.

All the old expressions are true—my heart was really pounding in my throat. Beads of sweat mixed with rain. I was soaked, concentrating, determined to make no movements at all—snaking, slipping through the last few vital yards. I could see nothing; it was all planned from way back there.

No snorts of slight alarm. The silence was overwhelming. I was pretty sure the group was still at hand. My whole nervous system channeled down to the machinery in my grip. I was a dot behind it. It was everything. The manic collector inside me took full charge—a starving demon with single-minded purpose.

Years of patience were invested in this dire crawl . . . right up against aeons of evolutionary hypersensitivity just on the other side of the impenetrable foliage. Projected visions were racing through my head. Two frantic animals face to face, seeing nothing of each other, pinpointing their intensity, freaking, frightened, furious tension. Their desperate different needs heightened with every inch of closeness . . . coming together for what I knew was the closest anyone could ever get.

I was as far as I could go and as low to the ground as one could picture. I eyed the camera rest four feet up, on an Aberdare olive, horizontalized, forked, and waiting for the ready camera and the ready lens: 120 mm, f 3.5, $\frac{1}{125}$ of a second now, the distance guesstimated at fifteen feet, light a little darker.

I was going to put the camera up first and then follow up behind it, like Nguya would, so slowly that no movement could be seen. Up, up over my head, slower than slow . . . fingers cushioning the olive log . . . easing the camera imperceptibly up and over . . . finally resting steady . . . a lonely picture-box on its own in plain sight, no head yet.

Then me, hair first, molecule by molecule in a trance of slowness, creeping up the damp camera back . . . getting my left eye up to that magic-window viewfinder . . . holding back the seething anticipation, slowly getting there, index finger already slightly pressing down . . .

A red-brown face, full frame, before me. Massive eyes boring down the tunnel of my lens, flies crisscrossing in the forehead fur, zigzagging nervous paths. A fly across the eye. Eyelashes that big. No blink. Radar ears outstretched. Urgent receivers. Not a single sound. Total living sculpture.

I knew this was going to be the most intense, most pregnant life-long key moment of all my wildlife crawlings and stalkings. This was it: the ultimate collection of split second in a stream, one after the other, the only time such a sight could ever be, because the muffled shutter click would end it all like a rifle blast. Animals gone.

Thousands of miles of hills and valleys and stinging nettles for this single vision . . . the wildest sight on earth . . . right now. The rarest. The intensity of the furious flies, the giant eyes, the neck reaching forward, so much wildness . . . stretching the moment. Gambling out on the longest limb of chance, squeezing the shutter release . . .

Concentration, consternation, trepidation. Imagination. Exhilaration. *Click.*

The loudest ever heard. An Olympic starting gun. Thundering

explosive hooves. Crashing bush alive with frenzy—every direction, everywhere. Forget the four! There must be fifty or more, a huge herd, all around. None of them knowing why or what. Galo-Galo was pulling me, tugging me around the tree. *Haraka.* Hurry. *Fwata mimi.* Follow me. We raced off again, triumphant, now circling around.

Snorting the air, noses were blowing. Then a giant lion-sized coughing *BARK*, an explosion—like a buffalo bull, a lion, a leopard—brief, inquiring, a loud calling out. Nothing quite like it. The fearsome utterance sounded again, and then again. We pursued it, madly crazed. The forest cover got darker but the ground was open, with movement all around; the great bellow bark was just ahead. I checked the aperture: F 3.5 still in place. Speed down to ⅟₆₀ of a second. And then there it was in gargantuan silhouette: buffalo-sized, frozen in place, almost calm, the biggest blackest bongo bull in the forests of Africa. This was the high point of a thousand lives, a-million-to-one odds. Great blackness and sleekness and togetherness and gentleness in the darkest black baseball-sized eyes . . . looking right down at me, completely open without fear or malice of any kind. Visual poetry of vast composition, pouring muscle. Fluid, ready. Mighty.

The whole form filled my lens—the hunter's dream. *Click* and he disappeared into the moist darkness, an apparition.

I let the film advance on motor drive, left eye open. By now the herd was out of sight. Deep silence restored. In my left eye the rewind spool remained unmoved, unturned, unbelievable . . . It hit me like a flash through the stomach, aching emptiness and despair—a searing pain— *the film was not turning in the camera.* Try the shutter, wind it, crank it, bang it—*nothing moves.* I would have to wait till dark to look inside and feel for torn film, sprockets probably ripped. Had I missed the goggle-eyed face of flies? Mind searching for reason with groans of darkest hope. From mountain peaks of ecstasy my mood began to match the gloomy forest. I'd got nothing and I knew it.

Time for desperate action. Grab the other camera from bewildered Galo-Galo. Change the lenses, run through the forest, find the herd. Find any one of them. Reach the next ridge, lungs on fire. Go for it. Quietly now . . .

Galo-Galo came up behind. We were all there. You could feel it. Forms were flowing through the bush, slightest rustlings here and there. We would see nothing, though. *@#%^&4@>$@<4@!!+=) [@}} {#!!

It was darkening now—at the very end of the afternoon. Below me in a vast stretch of primeval forest canopy cover was a single gap of low-lying bush, a clearing of sorts. We watched for anything that moved.

Just when I was despairing over why old Mungu couldn't throw us down a single crumb, just when I was really beyond hope and knew all was lost . . . the great elegance appeared in that one and only waist-high clearing . . . barely glancing in our direction, easing by, on his own time. Never a sound, back in the flow, heading up to the left . . . a sleek bongo.

One last glorious chance. *Click*. Check the rewind spool, open eyed. It winds . . . Got you!

And here he is, a male bongo, in the wild. Over the years, no one has even noticed this picture. No one knows what it is. No one could ever guess the months and years of trouble that lay behind it.

"*Shauri ya Mungu.*" Don't make too much effort. It's all God's plan.

ON THE RUN

The long good-bye. See you later, alligator. Don't kill yourself. Have a good one. Don't be a stranger. Take it real easy. Ciao. *Sayonara.* Bye now. *Kwaheri.* So long, pal. I gotta run. Be good. And don't take any wooden nickels, okay? Keep me posted. Regards to the family. Keep the faith. Have a nice day. Don't work too hard. Be well. Toodle-ooo. Get goin', will ya? Get outta here! In a while, crocodile. It's been great knowing you. And as they say in Kenya, "See-ya-just-now" or "You-know-where-we-live." Africa *addio.*

It's *so hard* to finish up. Deadlines are vital—before the deadly end. You really want to squeeze everything in before closing time—a notion in the back of your head about instant death falling in the night, or tumbling downhill at noon under a burning sun in long grass. Right up to that last minute jamming in all the extras, all your favorite little things, all the goodies, quotes, poems, proverbs, last-minute thoughts, advice to all. A whole world of beauty and truth. Art itself, summarized and tidied up for all to see. But it's so hard to begin the end, and usually we wait around until it's too late and it all gets done for us. Gulp. (*Shauri ya Mungu.*) This happened to me last September when I couldn't finish up Zara's book, and an extra-angry adult elephant from Tarzania showed me the way. The hard way.

An adventure, a landscape, a portrait, a song, a book, a life . . . Just a series of sensations, as Ulysses S. Grant (the American Civil War general and U.S. President No. 18) said of history: "Just one goddamned thing after another." Nevertheless, please, believe me, only too much is enough. Very naturally we want it all. We come from nothing and we go into nothing with lots of hope and denial. So we should absolutely want more and more, forever and ever. But just *now*, this little thing taking place right now is the only thing happening, so let's get more and more out of *it*. There it is, in a nutshell, this chapter and all of life itself, the big game played out for no ungreedy reason in the here and now somewhat selfishly. (Yes, I'm sorry. That's more or less all there is to it.) All the Latin homework and all the puffed-up propaganda they make you memorize at school comes from poorly informed adults ("He who can, does. He who cannot, teaches"—G. B. Shaw) and of course exceptions prove the rule).

> When I think back
> On all the crap I learned in high school
> It's a wonder
> I can think at all
> And though my lack of education
> Hasn't hurt me none
> I can read the writing on the wall
> —PAUL SIMON, "Kodachrome" (fittingly enough)

At the same time, don't forget, you get out of life what you put into it—or what you jam into it. "You never know what is enough unless you know what is more than enough" (William Blake). So keep on jamming, if for no other reason than to thicken up your one and only life, adding texture and bulk to the daily/yearly calendar, and possibly even coming up with something new. Yes, if you crave something new, something original, particularly when they keep saying "Less is more," remember that I say: Too much is really *just fine.* Only by going too far can we break the boring mold and stumble into something a little different. Originality is a key goal for the old human nervous system. In short, something new from something old—(old and in a rut).

The biggest and best homework assignment in life and art, and I'll give it to you right now, is to keep yourself excited, going *forward,* happy, *enthusiastic.* Look it up in a large etymological dictionary (even if you think you know what it means): eagerness, warmth, fervor, zeal, ardor, passion, devotion, having a god within.

With all this in mind, I sought medical advice from a Masai medicine man at the top of the Loita Hills, over eight thousand feet in altitude near a place called Tintamapia, or Magic Wood, just beyond the Valley of the Loibons. Loibons are Masai witch doctors who roll out the stones and the bones and smoke magic elephant-tusk pipes to divine

Loibon Taiyana at the grave of his father (Ol Lenana) on top of the Ngong Hills

the future (the hidden art of the Masai—the witch doctor's bones). They defy what we currently know about physics and math. They are the seers. They seem to possess all the truths of nature, they appear to see things with unusual clarity. They can help you. The Masai loibons are from a long line of mystics, working in other dimensions of reality, performing dark miracles and predictions and unexplainable cures in their gloomy, smoke-filled doctors' offices made of cow dung, and with lots of cattle in the living room—or, in my case, outside, in the rarified air, because my doctor was up at eight thousand feet on the very top of the Loitas, overlooking a large, lush view of photogenic Africa, including a patch of savannah stretching down below where I was about to get skewered by an enraged adult elephant. And therefore here are the very first pictures ever taken of these sacred Masai pipes, never before seen or heard of in the history of African art and artifacts, against a background of tall grasses where suddenly my whole life was forced to flash in front of me.

It was not like they say when you're falling off a precipice or something like that and your whole life appears in front of you at high speed on flash cards that flip through your mind. For me it was more like a tube of simple white toothpaste suddenly squeezed, and your whole life is exposed from the inside dark places out into the open, like an open deadline, squeeze, plunk, help, this is urgent. (The whole thing took about two weeks from my three days of consultation with the loibon.) He had covered me with powders, and he smoked both his magic pipes, which he insisted were "alive," both indoors and out, smoking and blowing powders and shaking and rolling stones from his age-old gourd. He never actually spelled anything out, but he was very busy the whole time, and he looked at me with promises of a lot to come. He was extremely abusive of the government officials in Nairobi who pooh-poohed the legitimacy of Masai medicine men's tools of trade—medicinal artifacts, works of art, national treasures really. And he was very aware that the government was openly burning ivory and rhino horn in their misguided political approach to so-called conservation. Bonfires of vanity and publicity. He said the whole future was endangered. Blowing his nose with two fingers, squeezing together either side. Then a good fast spit.

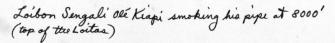

Loibon Sengali' Olé Kiapi smoking his pipe at 8000'
(top of the Loitas)

It was a powerful three days with the loibon. He was a gentle, elderly man with a big smile, and everything out in the open. No mumbo jumbo or scary stuff, except for excited spitting in the direction of the city. He concentrated very hard. And when he looked over at me, it was with long and provocative heavy eye contact, heavy staring. He rolled out the stones and arranged them in surprising piles and shook his head quite a bit. The Masai translator, who sat next to him, interpreted everything. Interestingly, he had never seen the sacred, secret pipes before. Only one favorite wife and the eldest son are allowed to touch these magic, living tools of the trade. And, throughout history, there is only one European reference to one rhino-horn pipe in Masailand, at the turn of the century, by the German anthropologist Moritz Merker. But after all, secrets are an important part of all art, especially this hidden art of the Masai.

It was Monday, September 9, 1996. High noon. My day and hour of reckoning had come—when all the toothpaste would come out of the tube and lie there in the grass by an anthill like an infinitesimal ant, a squishy, gooey, bloody ant. 9.9.96 . . . after forty-one years of pursuing elephants from every angle and every distance, there I was, caught out in the open without even a camera to record the stress-ridden calamity, the mayhem, the raging resentment, and the ant antics. I was with fourth-generation professional hunter Calvin (Curly) Cottar, son of Glen Cot-

Masai lion hunt

Mrs. Charles Cottar   Glen Cottar   Mike Cottar
Photograph by Charles Cottar

tar, my best friend in Kenya, who got nailed by a buffalo very nearby in 1964 when I was booked to go on safari with him. Glen was the son of Mike Cottar, who collected most of the trophies in the Field Museum in Chicago. And Mike was the son of Charles Cottar, who came from Cottar's Creek, Texas, to Kenya on the heels of Teddy Roosevelt's 1909 safari. But on this day generations of pedigree and experience made no difference.

We were out on a carefree picnic in Mike Cottar's old hunting block on the old Tanganyika border below the Loita Hills in Masailand, where Calvin had a vintage 1920s Karen Blixen–type campsite. With Mike Cottar's safari boxes and vintage equipment, including colonial Africa staff uniforms, it was a time warp. "I don't think of the past. The only thing that matters is the everlasting present . . ."

Who knows what human encroachment, cutting down of trees, plowing and planting, has led to local crop damage by hungry, rambunctious animals; and then Game Department "control work" (punishment shootings promised by politicians, usually carried out at night, firing into social units of already highly stressed elephants). In the 1990s human population pressure was relentlessly squeezing down on the elephants. Calvin had hardly seen any elephants here, but there they stood, a herd of about fifteen cows and calves silhouetted along the horizon of a hillside two hundred or three hundred yards away. "If we walk along with them for a while, they may go right into our camp," Calvin remarked optimistically and with considerable humor. I was following behind with my hands behind my back when the matriarch (lead cow) spun around and gave us a downhill demo—a raging, inflated demonstration to remind us to keep our distance. We ran back appropriately until she returned to the now excited herd, but we had stopped running too soon. Around she came again, trumpeting loudly with yet another downhill demo. Again we ran, trying to keep a good distance, until she would settle down and go off again with her herd. Run, run, run. "I feel it coming . . . I feel it coming . . . over my left shoulder . . . the primitive horror." Every few moments I glanced over my left shoulder, ready to slow down and rest. No such luck. This was turning into a bummer. Whether it was the downhill advantage, or the downhill in quality of life (stressed-out elephant life), we will never know. But this maniacal cow was bent way out of shape—heavy stress. Her trumpeting heads-up demo now had the head down, scraping the grassy ground—a deadly strategy, as if to cow-catch all of humanity with her greedy ivory teeth. They were just about the size of loibon Sengali olé Kiapi's magic smoking pipe, and they were getting closer and closer. For a second I even thought about olé Kiapi and his amazing intensity—then, at a certain point, Calvin and I split to make it a fifty-fifty choice for the angry matriarch. I went left and he went right. He was right. I got the lumbering pachyderm right on my tail. This was going to be it. No cover in sight—only a pathetic anthill up ahead. I never felt more like an ant, a particularly embarrassed ant.

A dumb ant, desperately concentrating on running without falling, running through the long Francis Bacon grass with hopeful backward glances, knowing now that this was it. No escape. It wouldn't take long, but there was plenty of time to feel like a fool. After so much of this over the years, to suddenly, rudely, discover how humans can get away with

just so much, time and again, until one day the dénouement, the ultimate snafu. They surely deserve their just deserts for pushing and pushing so far. Frantically retreating now, running back and away, too little too late, caught out, suspended between tension and collapse, horror, wait-and-see pudding . . . Relentless, flowing, squealing enormity, all downhill. Silent, pouring down on me—the unlucky ant.

An absurd speck in the long grass with bug legs, the grandeur of human futility, all alone now in the great Pleistocene landscape, epitomizing the human comedy, scampering to nowhere before this looming, lunatic mother, like Mother Nature herself, injured, insulted, insolent, incensed, impossible to change anyone's mind, impossible to stop . . . *Ahhhhhhh!*

Everything was going into my run. Baggy blue trousers stuffed with clippings and Tusker beer labels weren't helping. I thought of peeling off my shirt and throwing it back to confuse or somehow divert the attack. It was a smelly old shirt. It might have worked but the procedure was too much to pull off. Nevertheless I remember it as my last thought before the anthill. Perhaps I had a few others, but it's pretty hard to remember when everything's coming down the way it was. Zara, Hog Ranch, far-off friends. It was like entering one of those new dimensions, a kind of quiet lonely panic when you've only got yourself and the horrible thing that's heading your way. It was a little bit like as a child when I used to wonder what came before the universe, all the galaxies, stars, and planets. What came before the space that held all those materials inside? Mount Everest, etc. And then, *what came before that*, etc.? Hopeless questions that produced a hollow ache in the stomach.

Last thoughts before the anthill, the little, cementlike ant home for the exhausted ant to throw himself behind and cower there in the black-green shadows, out of breath, resigned, ridiculous, and small. And then the overwhelming reality hit hard. Down in the dirt, round and round, scrunched and pushed around in the dirt. For a few seconds her front leg was in my arms. *Phhhyyyhhh!* Then the head came down like a freight elevator crunching chicken bones. *Snap, snap.* Hips and ribs. You could plainly hear them under the squeezing pressure. Then it stopped. The other elephants came round with gurgling communications, rumbling like conversations. Curious sniffs from eager trunks. Sniffing and shuffling. Shuffling feet. Dusty, swishing, noisy, guttural greetings all around me, sniffing out the loser. One down, five billion to go.

Then they were gone.

I could hear a Land Cruiser engine heading my way, but all was black. My eyesight had been squeezed out. I tried to prop myself up a bit, to look less bad. My middle was completely crushed. Only arms worked. It was totally futile.

"Take off your pants, take off your pants," I heard the cry. "Get his pants down." This seemed a funny idea. I tried to point out my rib and hip section, assuring Calvin repeatedly that no tusk had gone through my legs. "*I would have felt it.* Just the head, *crunch*, just the head crunched me. No tusk . . . " But I was blind—and wrong. After a minute, looking right up into the noonday sun, which was dark black, the most fascinating thing began to occur. Not in front of my eyes, but inside them. Starting in the left one a sort of deep-down digital nightmare, *bleep-bleep*, like when the storm clouds recede from your thundered-out television satellite dish, TV screen. *Bleep-bleep*, little digital squares reappearing and popping back and joining like IBM bricks in a regulation jigsaw puzzle screen, finally forming a picture, a reality in the darkness. Left eye first. Then, like a good robot, the right eye began its digital recovery. Blink, blink, *ping*. And then there, in front of me, was a complete picture: worried faces peering down. I aimed my refurbished lenses downward, and there for all to see was a great, gaping, fist-sized hole speared through the khaki-blue trousers of my left thigh . . . In one side and out the other (never felt a thing). In the heat of the moment my mind must have blocked off this key event. Thank you.

By some kind of miracle the pipe-sized tusk had missed my femoral artery and the large nerve that if severed would have finished my leg in terms of feeling and further use, not to mention bleeding out rather quickly. Now the question was, what sort of smashed hips and ribs were bleeding inside? Hips bleed a lot when they're broken. There was no way to move. I was all broken up.

Lots of hands underneath me got the mangled carcass into the backseat of the Land Cruiser, and Calvin Cottar began the drive of his life and mine, with his left hand holding the wheel and his right one on the radio, radioing for help. Radioing someone to radio someone in Nairobi to get help from the Flying Doctors. Rocks, ditches, ruts, and anthills. He negotiated them all for miles. I could feel the slurping blood lapping against the inner walls of my body cavity. We bounced along, radioing and driving wildly (brilliantly) around obstacles. You can't really write about these things because morbid pains of this nature are not describable. But Zara later learned an exact duplication of this event and would writhe around on the floor moaning and groaning at anyone's request.

It took four hours to get to Nairobi Hospital. The biggest break came in the AMREF airplane. Morphine. The faces of the drivers and pilots and those who helped me inside the backseat will be with me for life. It was a sensory overload on the very edge of survival. As the AMREF ambulance pulled into Nairobi Hospital, I bled out in the driveway and was wheeled into Emergency on the dead list. How they stopped the bleeding and got all the bones back together I'll never know. I woke up the next day encased in a kind of steel structure that was screwed into my bone parts, and somehow all came together like an erector set. Seven pints of new blood had been pumped into my system. Authentic African blood . . . an initiation of sorts. Conservation techniques in surgery seem to exceed those in the wildlife preserves.

One year and quite a few operations later, and this book-ending chapter finally achieved, I was hobbling around with seven titanium plates and twenty-eight screws inside me. I learned that Nature is much bigger than all of us, and when you push too far it snaps back in your face. "Be bold, be bold . . . be not too bold"—one of Karen Blixen's mottos in her life.

My Kenya wildlife days were more or less terminated, but so, indeed, was wildlife in Kenya. . . . The end of the game, as it were. As I look back at the thought-filled stares of the loibon, Sengali olé Kiapi;

the stones, the bones, and the silent, serious people around him; the elephant-ivory pipe and the one that went right through me, so many summary calculations flood my mind, I can only try to sum them up, and you'll have to trust my math.

At first I thought the loibon was wasting my time and then I thought he was wrong. His steady, staring optimism forecast so much for me, it looked like a large joke from the bloody stretcher. But I was wrong to judge so soon. Yes, it was the nudge I needed.

Hello, anyone there? *Knock, knock*. High time for a wake-up call. The Asian *duka* sign said it all: *"May heaven's choicest blessings be showered upon you."* Every single day from September 9, 1996, till now has been loaded with positive feedback that would never have occurred in my trudging, rutted, worn-down life of unfinished busyness—unfilled, unprinted twenty million negatives, unwritten words. Just as the loibon indicated. As Karen Blixen put it: "Africa amongst the continents will teach it to you: *God and the Devil are one—the majesty co-eternal."* There seems to be an accountant up there somewhere who knows which way the ivory pipe blows, and olé Kiapi holds one of the pipes. The truth really does come in the strangest door, and sometimes you have to go blind before you can see it.

You don't know when you've had enough till you've had too much, you can't begin a decent ending until you open up your eyes and see what's been going on before. Huge balances are at work. We are not in charge. The winner of the final chapter may not be the suave, modern-day, technologically advanced Blade Runner Future Man of the World Wide Web, with clones and digitalized robots looming in the pride-filled future, air-conditioned with duplication factors, Erector-set robots on the assembly line, atomic advancements in pollution-free smokestacks and nuclear waste disposal. New methods of cleaning up the spills. Desperate new cures for new kinds of cancer, heart disease, Ebola, Zaire, SARS, and every pest sent to us by NATURE herself.

Olé Kiapi, in his lofty cow-dung shelter, may have access to more answers than all of our speedy, high-tech, modern-day laptop-computer manipulators, who, like agents of *the galloping rot* itself, jeopardize the world of nature and the age-old diversity of nature's timeworn secrets. The dark world he represents is far older, far more practical, down-to-earth, and it has survived many millions of years longer than the computer systems that threaten our racing existence and his existence.

The faster and farther we go from nature, the more we seem to lose: not just crocodiles and elephants, but the whole diversity package. The intertwined, symbiotic complexities of the wild-deer-ness, whose fitness and uniqueness enable survival, just can't ever be repeated. How much better the scaly creatures (reptiles and pachyderms) you know, than the scaliness you don't know. Slowly, slowly we corner ourselves with machinery on miles and miles of cement that paves over and robs the value from our one and only habitat, bleeding the common sense out of our being. This is the question in my mind, the question I am leaving with you: Will the machines in the emergency rooms be able to save us from ourselves? From our clones, our robots, our diseaselike cities and suburbs, spreading like a really active virus? We pray so. An old plaque on a grave in the Ngong Hills puts it clearly: "He prayeth well who loveth well, Both man and bird and beast."

THE END

Acknowledgments

Hog Ranch Art Department, E. Mwangi Kuria, Solimon Mkosia, Peter Malimbi, Gabriel Macharia Mwangi, George Mugai Gitau, Nicholas Njenga, Tabitha Kutayi, Mbuno, Kamante Gatura, Galo-Galo Guya, Meriel Destro, Nathenial Kivoi, Maina Mwangi, and to David Gulden, Vicky Wilson, Keith Keller, Gigi Johnson, Steve Aronson, Linda Fiske, and Nejma Beard.

A NOTE ON THE TYPE

The text of this book was set in Van Dijck, a modern revival of a typeface attributed to the Dutch master punchcutter Christoffel van Dyck, c. 1606–69. The revival was produced by the Monotype Corporation in 1937–38 with the assistance, and perhaps over the objection, of the Dutch typographer Jan van Krimpen. Never in wide use, Monotype Van Dijck nonetheless has the familiar and comfortable qualities of the types of William Caslon, who used the original Van Dijck as the model for his famous type.

Composition and color separations by
North Market Street Graphics, Lancaster, Pennsylvania
Printed and bound by Tien Wah Press, Singapore
Designed by Peter A. Andersen